WICCA

WICCA

A MODERN GUIDE TO WITCHCRAFT & MAGICK

Harmony Nice

SEAL PRESS

Seal Press
Hachette Book Group
1290 Avenue of the Americas, New York, NY 10104
sealpress.com
@SealPress

Printed in the United States of America

First published in Great Britain in 2018 by Orion Spring, an imprint of The Orion Publishing Group Ltd.

Published by Seal Press, an imprint of Perseus Books, LLC, a subsidiary of Hachette Book Group, Inc. The Seal Press name and logo is a trademark of the Hachette Book Group.

The Hachette Speakers Bureau provides a wide range of authors for speaking events. To find out more, go to www.hachettespeakersbureau.com or call (866) 376-6591.

The publisher is not responsible for websites (or their content) that are not owned by the publisher.

Illustrations by Laura Shelley at www.laurashelleydesign.com

Library of Congress Cataloging-in-Publication Data has been applied for.

ISBNs: 978-1-58005-915-2 (hardcover), 978-1-58005-914-5 (ebook)

LSC-C

10 9 8 7 6 5 4 3 2 1

To my best friend Morena,
strong witch; stronger and most valuable, irreplaceable friend.

My family,
To my mother Jade, without whom this book would not have been possible, Peter, Isabella and Genevieve (and the rest of them). My crazy family, close as a family, but even closer as friends.

Yvonne,
the highs were better with you; the lows will always be harder without you.

To the others,
loving boyfriend and incredible friends, where without them, the flowers would look less beautiful and the world would be so much less enjoyable. The many Witches & Wiccans I have encountered who have changed my path and my life, including my Inspirations, Scott Cunningham, Tituba, Stevie Nicks, Marie Laveau. Not to mention my closest Wicca friends, Georgia Burns, eclectic solitary Wiccan and the lady who has educated me on Wicca for the last four years, former Gardnerian Wiccan, current Faery Wiccan, who wishes not to be named. Last but not least, Anais Alexandre, the powerful Afro-Wiccan who was kind enough to share her information on Afro-Wicca and educate me on her path.

Contents

My Story

I was born on 19 May 1997, in a small town in Norfolk, England. My mother and father, Jade and Peter, both worked hard to provide me and my two sisters with a loving, noisy family home. According to my parents, I was a calm and cute baby, and for whatever reasons, I grew into a nutty child – the sort who couldn't sit still, spent most of the time mixing up mud pies in the garden and didn't ever want to be told what to do.

I didn't really enjoy primary or high school. I wasn't bullied, and I didn't really have a hard time, but I just wasn't very good at the subjects that we were taught, except for the few that I loved, Drama, English and Biology. I've heard some people say that they knew what they wanted to do with their lives when they were very young, but I didn't. I knew there was something more to life – just what that was, I didn't know.

When I was fourteen, I remember lying outside in the summer in my front garden with my mum and asking her about her family. Mum told me stories about her grandma, Maud, a kind and creative woman whose family owned a flower nursery, and with whom my mother spent a lot of her childhood, painting, baking and playing games.

For the first time, she spoke about my great-grandmother, Hilda. My curiosity was instantly piqued. Hilda was a half-German witch; she made fur coats, played with Ouija boards and cast spells on people to give them headaches when they annoyed her – so, basic-ally nothing like the type of witch I am. This was the first time that I realised witchcraft was real; magick was real.

Even though I've never met these incredible women, somehow I feel connected to them both. After these conversations, it felt like a switch had been flicked in my brain. Yes, I'd had interests before – I had dabbled in hobbies, had a go at playing various musical instruments, become a bit obsessed with dyeing my hair every colour under the sun and even read up on Buddhism – but each time I grew bored and gave up.

Witchcraft was different. I began reading up on it, and over the next few months gradually learned about the different types of witches, spells and crafts, about necromancy, divination, the lot. I purchased my first set of tarot cards soon after and began tarot reading. I also started doing witchcraft. I'm cringing now – at how I had no idea what I was doing and I most certainly made mistakes – but all of this was a great learning curve for the future. I'd love to say the rest is history – I found my way and that was it – but that would be far from the truth.

My paternal grandmother, Yvonne Nice, had passed away suddenly in the previous year. Looking back, this affected me so much more than I realised at the time. We were all incredibly close to her; she had a fun-loving, larger-than-life personality, and her death left our family in a mutual state of shock for a long time. The combination of my grief and the fact that I was also dealing with a lot of other, typical adolescent stresses was probably the trigger for a long, difficult period of depression. This lasted for most of my teenage years. I also experienced a couple of negative and damaging relationships, the effects of which had severe repercussions on my mental health – resulting in self-harm, anxiety and finally dissociation. It wasn't an easy ride, but, with hindsight, I didn't make things easy for myself. My negativity and jealousy were through the roof; I was unkind and confused, and didn't really give much thought to anyone else. No wonder I was so unhappy.

This period lasted longer than I care to mention, but things did improve. There was no simple fix that stimulated my recovery; it took a long time and a lot of help from many angels. As things began to improve, in 2014, I created my first YouTube video, 'Kylie Jenner Make-up Tutorial'. As you can see, my content has changed direction slightly. I started going out more and began to try and find a purpose. Obviously, life still had its ups and downs after that, but

I continued to get better. The challenging aspects of my life, such as relationships, got easier to deal with. I felt as though I had the ability to get through negative times, which I hadn't had before.

There was one day in particular that changed everything for me. I was browsing in a second-hand bookshop in Norwich, when I came across *Living Wicca* by Scott Cunningham. I had heard of Wicca before, but never looked into it, and was under the popular misconception that a Wiccan was some kind of good witch (see page 14 for the differences between Wicca and witchcraft). Scott would become my inspiration and guide for 80 per cent of everything I've ever done in my Wicca journey.

At this point I hadn't really touched witchcraft for a few months and it seemed like a distant part of me. I didn't purchase the book then, but the drawing on the cover caught my eye. It was a picture of a red-haired lady, holding her hands in the air either side of a goddess symbol. I got home that day, lay on my bed and typed the words into my phone: 'What is Wicca?' Yes – as typical as it sounds – that moment marked another beginning for me.

I began my Wicca journey, trying to learn something new about the faith every day. Nothing seemed to get in the way at this point. Wicca made me ask myself, what makes you happy? What makes you unhappy? It changed the way that I saw everything.

I decided to clear out anything and anyone in my life that worked against my happiness or had a destructive effect on my self-worth. I also decided to apologise and make good any harmful acts that I felt I had committed towards others. I stopped tweeting about people – using negative force to fight my unhappiness – stopped speaking behind people's backs, stopped using social media as a platform to validate myself and, instead, started trying to be myself.

Wicca soon became something that I wanted to dedicate my life to. It has brought me many benefits. I learned acceptance, kindness and self-love. Therapy made a significant contribution to supporting my mental health, but learning about Wicca and dedicating my life to the faith helped me to see the amazing potential and compassion that surrounds us.

I started my journey as an eclectic solitary Wiccan when I was seventeen, and I honestly feel that from that day everything improved: my friendships, my relationships, my morals, my creativity, my mental health. My faith helped me to accept things; even in difficult times I still feel at one with the universe. About a year later, I performed my ceremony of self-dedication to Wicca. Before you ask, I was very fortunate in that my parents had no problems with what I was doing. In fact, I think that my mother was happy that my interests were in something that benefitted my attitude and my health. Wicca felt like it was mine at that time; I didn't know anyone else who was Wiccan. I kept it all to myself for a long while, it felt so personal, and I think that this allowed me to develop a strong bond with the faith.

My YouTube channel was slowly flourishing, with the number of my followers beginning to rise, and one day I decided to mention in a video that I practised something called Wicca. The response that I got was overwhelming – literally thousands of people asking me to talk about the faith online and to help educate them and learn alongside them. I made my first 'Enchanted Endeavours' episode, a series on my channel which is still running two years later. The first episode was about crystals, and a whole new part of my journey began.

I was now in communication with a worldwide community of Wiccans, with whom I continue to share a mutual educational journey. I have had so many fascinating conversations about Wicca because of this, including with one particular practitioner, who has over thirty years' experience and has helped me open my eyes to new elements and not just to stick to one path. It was after this conversation that I realised I'd never stop learning about Wicca and that just made me want to work harder – which is what I'm doing still. I think that one of the most important things I ever did in Wicca was make mistakes: mistakes help you grow – far more than your successes do. And here I am now – years later – a solitary Green Wiccan who is definitely still studying, and who probably will be forever.

Through my teaching and learning about Wicca on YouTube and in everyday life, it has become apparent that this is what I was meant to do. In these last four years, I have acquired the knowledge that I share in this book from so many different, amazing and inspirational people. I have also learned that there are many confusing and biased ideas about Wiccan teachings and practices. A few books that I have read now seem outdated and I have often felt that as a new Wiccan, starting my journey, I could have really benefitted from a book that explained the basics in a straightforward manner, without too much emphasis on rules!

I wanted to create this book for Wiccans of any age and length of experience. I hope that it is an honest and informative read that will minimise confusion, while also being fun, interesting and appropriate to the modern-day faith. I wanted to write about my struggles and mistakes and to dispel the common misconception that there is only *one* correct way to practise Wicca; because holy hell, there's not!

I want to help people who, like me, have Wicca inside them, to guide them into something that could be as beneficial, and feel as right to them, as it does for me.

Lots of love and light, Harmony x

▶ Harmony Nice
⚬ @peachycinnamon

Introduction:
Wicca for a Modern World

Paganism and witchcraft have been around longer than you could probably imagine, but in the last five years, Wicca has progressed in ways that Wiccans who practised in the 1960s, or even the 1990s, could never have imagined.

Witchcraft has a long history of persecution and misunderstanding. In the sixteenth century, even being suspected of practising it could lead to being punished by death. By the eighteenth century, however, witches had mostly come to be seen as frauds, and were fined or imprisoned for using witchcraft to con and frighten people.

By the twentieth century, Wicca was firmly established by secretive covens. At this stage witches were often perceived as crazy women, wearing pointed hats and capes, dancing naked around the fire! That began to change as films and TV shows – such – as *Bewitched*, *True Blood* and the Harry Potter franchise – fashion trends and an increasing number of books on and featuring witchcraft and Wicca fostered interest.

Witchcraft and Wicca are, importantly, quite distinct. Thankfully, there is a genuine interest in the real meaning, practices and values of Wicca. We are a nature-based religion; we live and breathe true kindness and compassion, empowering ourselves and others around us, worshipping elements of our earth such as the moon, the sun, the universe, nature and the magick that they bring to us. We teach tolerance and diversity and acceptance. Solitary or in a coven, a practising Wiccan for a year or fifty years; we live our faith and respect our earth. The magick we produce comes from within and around us, not from looking the correct way or having the fanciest tarot cards.

Popular culture has brought witchcraft into the public eye, with famous personalities such as musicians Stevie Nicks and Björk alleged to be involved in witchcraft. So, the combination of readily available accurate information and people in the public eye embracing witchcraft and Wicca has helped bring more acceptance. Society is realising that we do not promote evil concepts, using magick against people to turn them into frogs, but a peaceful way of life that benefits us and those around us. People from all backgrounds, cultures, races, genders and sexualities are finding their feet in Wicca, creating their free paths within the faith. They are discovering that it is a way to empower themselves and others and are using it to improve their lives. There is now nothing to fear and we can proudly announce to the world that we are Wiccans and witches!

Wicca is certainly a faith for all but more recently, especially over the last few years, it's opened a lot of eyes for many young women around the world. Wicca sparks creativity and allows people the choice to use elements of it to help them make their lives the way they want them to be. Lots of young girls are drawn to the faith because of the freedom and power it possesses. To me, it's a religion that promotes equality in all; one that hasn't been warped to suit one gender or race and has flexibility. Where some may feel trapped within other religions or even just in their everyday lives, Wicca can help break through those barriers.

Of course, with the changes that the internet has brought to humankind in the last couple of decades, Wicca has entered the online world, making it so much easier for everyone to learn. There are amazing communities of Wiccans, posting about spells, their journeys, Wicca teachings and even online covens. The answers to everything that you may be interested in or may have been wondering about are potentially just a few clicks away. There are some incredibly informative, experienced Wiccans writing online blogs, and you can access teachings from famous Wiccans which are documented online. For practical help, YouTube videos allow us to watch people carrying out their magickal workings, such as divination, spell and ritual work, which can be far more useful than just reading about the theory of these things. However, the downside with this accessible sharing of information is that anyone can publish online, so you have to be aware of occasional misinformation.

MODERN WAYS TO PRACTISE

To me, Wicca will always be about experiencing the earth, working with what you can find and practising the craft for its true meaning. That doesn't mean that we shouldn't embrace the amazing, positive aspects of what living in 2018 has brought to us.

First, as I mentioned previously, we can learn spells pretty much anywhere now. There are tons of spells, rituals and potions to make, adapt to our own intuition or use at our will, all documented online by experienced Wiccans. There are also an increasing number of books about spell work being published every year by incredible authors – not to mention the most accurate way of learning spells, from trusted witches and Wiccans.

It's also much easier now to find the tools that we may want to use in our practices and to research different types of tools and raw materials. We can order purpose-made athames and bolines (both ritual knives) and chalices for our altars if that is what we prefer. There are also many online shops now, selling an endless supply of tarot cards, wands, crystals and even herbs that you can order and import for all of your magickal needs. This may open up opportunities for us to create spells with elements that we could have never dreamed of twenty years ago.

Wicca is no longer a secret – and before the faith's recent growth in popularity, some practitioners may have felt it necessary to keep their activities confidential. Access to open discussion and education on the true meaning of Wicca has changed opinions on both personal and family levels and also in the media. The fact that we can (funds allowing!) relatively easily visit the ruins of the temples of ancient Rome, dedicated to our chosen deities, or that we can contact an online coven in another continent brings the possibilities of our practices, experiences, understanding and discussions to another level, if this is what we choose.

Everything is so easy to source and learn now; it's wonderful in so many ways, but it's important to remember that a faith based on authentic principles is far more important than making a fashion statement and how you are perceived on social media.

SOCIAL MEDIA FOR WICCANS

Social media has benefitted today's Wiccan community in extreme amounts and, without it, a *lot* of us would have never even heard of the faith. It's an incredible tool to use on our Wicca journeys. There are increasingly more Wiccans, witches and pagans educating people on YouTube; they are creating tutorials showing us how to cast specific spells, illustrating how to do divination and sharing many more personal aspects of their practices.

Instagram has also seen a new community come to light, with Wiccans either teaching or showing their followers aspects of their journey or simply enjoying the witch aesthetic that has become popular with the new wave of Wiccans online. There are also apps for pretty much anything, from tarot readings, to online spell books, to Wicca community pages for Wiccans to share and connect. In general, this is an extremely positive step forwards, but there are two sides to it. Yes – everything is easier and anything we want for our Wicca journeys, tools, herbs, information, etc., can be sourced easily and quickly. However, sometimes social media can affect people's journeys negatively and a lot of younger Wiccans may not see the faith for what it truly is. Wicca *is* a faith, a way of life; you don't need every tool or every herb, need to know every detail when you are starting out. Just because you have a crystal ball and someone else does or doesn't have the economic means or space to have one, that doesn't make you a better Wiccan.

The witch style, aesthetic and vibes are fun and the online communities are incredibly interesting and entertaining but, in reality *any* true Wiccan can live and breathe their Wicca paths with or without the internet. The foundation and beliefs of Wicca will always be as simple as they were fifty years ago. There are some things you can learn only from experience, living as a Wiccan every day. This knowledge gained from daily witchcraft and the secrets within Wicca cannot be found online.

The internet, used correctly, can be an incredible tool to help us with our practices and, as it's a huge part of our society, why not embrace it? There are so many incredible Wiccans, witches and pagans behind this movement, so do seek out the writers, the YouTubers and the platforms we use to share our journeys with the world as witches and Wiccans.

Part
1

What Is Wicca?

The Wicca faith, its traditions and principles can signify different things to different people and many aspects are open to interpretation. I have attempted to outline the basics as I understand them from my own experiences, study and day-to-day practices.

1.

Wicca, Witchcraft and Paganism

The most common confusion about the terms Wicca, witchcraft and paganism is the difference between them. I have often been asked whether all witches consider themselves to be Wiccans, and some people think that all pagans consider themselves to be witches and many people are under the misconception that to be a Wiccan just means to be a 'good' witch. There is a huge difference between the three, so let us clear up the difference now. This could also help you when thinking about which path to follow from the beginning and maybe discovering which one you consider yourself to be.

WICCA

Wicca is a pagan, nature- and witchcraft-based religion. A Wiccan is someone that follows pagan beliefs and also practises witchcraft as a part of their faith. We follow the eight Sabbats (festivals) and twelve Esbats (celebrations of the full moon) and practise magickal workings such as rituals and spell work at specific times related to the phases of the moon. A Wiccan follows the energy and power of the natural earth and the universe and all its natural occurrences, the moon, the sun and the stars.

Wicca also promotes a great sense of freedom and positivity. It gives you the opportunity to take a path in the faith that you feel is right for you, allowing you freedom within the faith to do things in a way that you choose. Wicca embraces the fact we all have different beliefs and opinions while still being a part of the faith; it gives us the opportunity to live how we would like to but with the guidelines of our beliefs. Wicca promotes positivity but also self-love and empowerment, while trying to diminish negative energy and behaviours. Most of all we believe in balance: we believe that there can be no good without bad and that we cannot learn if we do not make mistakes. We own our mistakes and realise we alone are in charge of our behaviour. Wiccans tend to have morals and codes that keep this balance in our lives and that ensure we are as kind to humans, animals and the earth as we can possibly be. This also means keeping cruel, manipulative and toxic behaviour towards others as far away from us as possible. Wiccans practise their magick using the natural world around them. This can be from the ingredients that they use, the earth's energy and even the timing of when we carry out our spell work, using the moon's phases and seasons to guide us. We incorporate magickal workings into our philosophy to keep harmful factors out of our lives and to bring in positivity and goodness.

PAGANISM

A pagan is simply someone who follows a nature-based religion, paganism. There are several religions that could fall under the term paganism, such as Wicca, Druidry and Asatru. Pagans can be monotheistic or polytheistic, which means they can believe in one or many divine beings. Many pagans believe in one god and one goddess as they tend to believe in balance. Pagans practise nature-worship (which may sound a little strange to you, but it's not, I promise). Many have a strong belief that the earth is sacred and they should treat it as an equal to themselves and take care of it as well as they possibly can. All of their practices follow the earth and natural occurrences such as the seasons, the moon and phases of the sun.

WITCHCRAFT

Last, but not least, is witchcraft. This is a practice. It is a craft. And a witch is somebody that practises witchcraft; to be specific, who practises magick and uses the earth's energy to achieve a specific desired result. Anybody who practises a form of magickal workings, such as divination and future prediction, healing using the natural world, ritual work, spells, potions, alchemy, herbalism, etc., can be considered a witch. Sometimes even people with psychic abilities or who are spiritual mediums may consider themselves to be witches. So, a witch is someone who simply practises witchcraft in some shape or form. This means you do *not* have to be a Wiccan to be a witch, nor do you have to celebrate the Sabbats or follow any pagan teachings: a witch can have any or no religion. This also means you can be considered a witch if you are a Wiccan, even though 'Wiccan' is the preferred term, because we practise witchcraft as an element of our path.

2.

Divination

Divination uses a variety of tools in order to gain insight into situations, or your own or other people's lives. Many Wiccans enjoy practising divination – it is a massive subject – and I get asked so many questions about it.

Wiccans use divination to predict the future, to gain insight into the present and the past. Sometimes in life you need a little help, maybe you're feeling confused about a situation or you want some insight into which path the situation is moving towards. By using divination, you are allowing messages to come to you by using tools in a specific way in order to hear guidance from the universe and the divine.

I believe that everybody has some kind of psychic ability, but most of us mask it unintentionally throughout everyday life. Divination can be a tool to unlock and exercise our psychic abilities, allowing them to shine through. Your subconscious psychic mind needs to take over, which can be extremely relaxing and make you feel close with the divine; it can also help you to balance your emotions.

Divination helps to bring the solutions to problems into the light. Some Wiccans prefer to stick with one form, while others like to explore and work with all methods. There are many incredible books and online resources that explain and demonstrate the different divination techniques. I would suggest researching the methods that most appeal to you and reading and watching as many tutorials as you can. Until then, here are some basics:

DIFFERENT METHODS OF DIVINATION

TAROT READING

Tarot cards are a deck of seventy-eight cards, twenty-two of which are the major arcana and the other fifty-six, the minor arcana.

The major arcana are the cards that you might have seen before, with the names at the bottom of the cards, for example 'The devil', 'The lovers', etc. These cards are typically seen as the stronger cards: you must take notice of these during your readings as they are cards for the long-term and are related to the more significant parts of your life.

The minor arcana are split up into four suits – the wands, the swords, the cups and the pentacles/coins. Each suit has fourteen cards. Each of the suits count from one to ten; the number one is usually represented as the 'ace' card and the suit also has a page, a knight, a king and a queen. The minor arcana are still important cards, but are perhaps more relevant to the short-term and to the background of your life situations. It's still important to treat these as significant as they can still impact on some major parts of your life. In a tarot card deck, each card symbolises something different, thoughts, feelings, situations and intentions all presented in each card. As you draw a card, it is telling you what it represents in relation to your life. There is a card for everything that a human can experience. Tarot card reading can give insight into the future, present and past. For me, the cards lay your life and the situations in your life out in front of you, making it easy to gain understanding and perspective.

You can also use tarot cards in your other magick, for instance, in guided meditation; if you are focusing on relationship problems you might want to hold or place the Lover's card in front of you. The tarot cards are made from organic materials and they collect energies in a similar way to the other tools that Wiccans use from the natural world. In the same way, you can use tarot cards for spell work; by choosing a card that relates to the spell that you are casting.

RUNE STONES

These are a set of stones, crystals, plastic or wooden pieces which have been painted, carved or engraved with ancient alphabetic symbols. A typical set has twenty-four stones, but can have as many as thirty, depending on where they are from. Sometimes each set includes a blank stone too. Most rune stones have the Elder Futhark alphabet written on them; each letter also symbolises significant power and meaning (see page 182). Some rune stones have different alphabets with different interpretations, but the stones with the Elder Futhark alphabet are the most commonly seen.

There are many ways to cast rune stones. One method is to either hold the stones in your hand or in a bag and draw stones one at a time, noting their meanings as you do so. Another way is to cast your rune stones into a cloth, a mat or a bowl.

Rune stones are known for having magickal and spiritual properties, you can use them for divination and guided meditation much like tarot cards and crystals. If you cast your rune stones and there is a stone in particular you would like to gain more insight into you can meditate with it too. You can also use rune stones for spell work.

Rune stones are also often used for protection purposes. The symbols can be used and painted around your homes, on your tools and in your Book of Shadows.

SCRYING

Scrying is the term for gazing into mediums with a reflective or polished surface such as crystal balls, water, scrying mirrors made from obsidian, or into fire or smoke. The art of gazing is an extremely powerful thing. It relaxes your mind and allows your psychic abilities to see visions, images and messages. These can give you insights into problems that you might be considering and can answer questions about the futures of yourself and others. You must let the images and visions come to you. Don't force it – it will come naturally with time and practice. These visions can be received in different ways; some people have them appear fairly clearly in their minds while gazing at the medium, some see visions in the reflections and others make out shapes and images within the medium that they are using – for example, in fire you could, briefly, see the face of someone familiar in the flames.

The best way that I have had scrying described to me is that it is similar to when you're lying in the dark, looking around your room, if you focus enough, you can organise what you see into shapes, objects and muted colours. Or you can do a similar thing if you close your eyes and concentrate on looking into the darkness behind your eyes.

Seeing a situation from the perspective of a reflection is very effective for use in meditation, necromancy and also accessing other realms. It is difficult to work with and can take some getting used to. Meditation is a wonderful way to relax you into your subconscious if this is easier for you.

PALMISTRY

Palmistry is the art of reading the lines on somebody's hand for divination and future prediction. The hands possess a large amount of power and their appearance can show us various different aspects of our lives and personalities. Each line, bend and mark, depending on the thickness and shape, has a different meaning. Different experiences in life are also represented, including career and relationships.

TASSEOGRAPHY

Tasseography is the art of reading tea leaves that are left in your cup after drinking the tea. You can work out shapes, pictures and symbols that you can interpret to predict the future. It's an ancient form of divination that can be practised with different mediums such as tea leaves, coffee grains and wine residue as well.

Tasseography is sometimes more difficult than other forms

of divination because you are relying solely on your psychic intuition to work out what is in the cup. However, with a bit of practice you will soon be using your knowledge and intuition to work out symbols and meanings in the leaves. For instance, seeing a skull can signify an ending or something to be wary of and a snake can indicate betrayal.

You can use any cup for tasseography, but a small, round, light-coloured teacup seems to be better for getting accurate readings and to see the tea leaves more clearly than you would with a mug. A cup with a saucer is ideal because during a tea leaf reading you need something to flip your cup onto to put the excess tea leaves on. You can also buy tasseography cups that work in a slightly different way, with symbols around the cup so that the area that the tea leaves settle in is relevant to your reading.

PENDULUMS

Pendulums are one of the oldest, most incredible forms of divination, used in so many aspects of Wicca and spell work. A pendulum is typically a chain or string with a crystal or a wooden or metal pointed charm attached to the end. It is an extremely simple method of divination used to gain information by receiving answers, depending on how the pendulum swings. You have to train your pendulum to work by clasping the top of it in your hand and asking it to say 'no', then recording how it says 'no', asking it to say 'yes' and recording that action too. You may have to do this a few times to get the pendulum tuned to you and to make sure it's performing in a consistent way for each 'yes' and 'no' answer. Once you've trained the pendulum and understood its movements, you have bonded and can use it to ask questions and gain insight into situations. You can also use a pendulum chart for your divination work. As well as being a relatively simple form of divination, it is also inexpensive and very versatile!

3.

Nature

Nature is everything to Wiccans. Nature is the basis behind our practices; it is everything that we believe in, live by, worship, use and honour. Nature is all around us, everything that the earth has produced, natural occurrences, weather, the trees, the grass, plants, animals, the stars, the seas, the moon and the sun.

The earth owes us nothing; humans do not own the earth; neither are they more important. The earth is here with us – and in Wicca we work alongside nature. We love the earth and help it, respect it and honour it as much as we can. To Wiccans, the natural world is like a church is to Christians. Nature made us; we all evolved from the same place. In nature, everything has found its own natural balance and in Wicca, we strive to do the same within ourselves. This is why we treat everything as equal and respect that everything should maintain a balance. We also realise that nothing is perfect; there can be no good without bad, no dark without light and no birth without death.

Wicca teaches equality, love and tolerance; it doesn't matter who you are, where you come from, your race, gender or sexuality. Everything and everyone evolved from the same place; the earth and the natural world that created us; we all exist in the same universe and without every individual living thing, the world would not have balance.

Over the last centuries, science has made so many break-throughs and discovered many amazing things, such as the Big Bang theory, cures and prevention of diseases and various energy sources that we now take for granted – which are all incredible, aren't they? Yes, all of these things have been proven or developed by science, using our earth's natural reserves and properties, but this doesn't make them any less magickal. The natural world has so much incredible potential – and magick and witchcraft use some of the earth's capacity to push boundaries and discover ways to heal, help, create and communicate. Nature produces medicines and plants that have proven effects on our body. For instance, you can eat fungi that make you have visions (I don't recommend this!), you can drink camomile tea to calm an upset stomach or rub lavender oil on your forehead to help you sleep. Early practitioners of witch-craft were damned and seen as evil, but they were herbalists who combined natural materials to benefit and heal; their potions were early medicines. Everything that the human race has ever discov-ered comes from the natural world; it's all already here. It some-times just requires us to open our eyes so that we can see it.

HOW DO WE EMBRACE NATURE?

So, how do you incorporate the natural world into your Wicca journey? Like I said, it's the basis for everything that Wiccans believe. We celebrate the seasons and the moon phases (see Part 3, Wiccan Holidays and the Wheel of the Year) and we use natural materials in our practices. We welcome and support nature by studying and learning as much as we can about the natural world and how we can use crystals, herbs, plants, trees, water, snow, rain, the moon, the sun, etc. In fact, my favourite and the easiest recom-mendation is embrace nature when you are starting out in Wicca. Go outside – go for a walk, for a swim in a lake, pick some flowers, plant some seeds, feel the elements, really think about your experi-ences and write about how these things make you feel. Nature has provided everything that we have, we simply wouldn't be here without it! Celebrate what it has given us. Don't take advantage of the power that we have to destroy it. Try your best and embrace every second you have with it. Work alongside nature to benefit your life and to assist the earth. Every day the sun rises and the cycle of life continues, where would we be without it?

4.

The Three-Fold Law, Morals and the Wiccan Rede

As we have discussed, the Wicca path is typically a super free one – and this is one of the factors that makes Wicca so special. But that does not mean that Wiccans can do whatever they please without a care for anyone else. Of course not! Within Wicca, we have moral principles and laws that keep us on the Wiccan path and that encourage a positive, kind and thoughtful lifestyle.

THE THREE-FOLD LAW

The Three-Fold Law, also known as the law of three, is a moral guide for some Wiccans; it's a kind of Wicca form of karma. The basic belief of the Three-Fold Law is: whatever energy you send out into the earth, you will get back three times over.

Some Wiccans interpret this as the positive or negative will return to them three times and others believe that whatever type of energy they send out into the universe will have an effect on the three major parts of their own being – physically, emotionally and spiritually.

Not all Wiccans follow the Three-Fold Law, but most Wiccans believe in the basic principle that whatever energy you put into the earth, be it negative or positive, it will return to you. For example, if you are a Wiccan who practises positivity and respect throughout their life and also in their Wiccan practices, you send out a lot of positive energy and this positivity should return to you. I, personally, think that this is true, regardless of whether you believe in the Wicca faith. Think about it this way, if you spend your time being unkind, writing passive-aggressive tweets or statuses, making harsh or hurtful indirect comments or, in general, are super negative to those around you, chances are people will legitimately not enjoy your company and may not want to be associated with you. This could lead to you being alone and not feeling respected, which will inevitably give you negative emotions and affect your life in a potentially damaging way. Again, whether or not you believe in the spiritual side of this principle, there is something here for us all to reflect on.

During magickal workings, it is crucial to remember this way of thinking and to bear in mind that a lot of (all though not all) Wiccans live their spiritual, mental and physical life by the saying from the Wiccan Rede (see pages 30–1), 'An Ye Harm None, Do What Ye Will'. In a modern form, this is, 'If it harms none, do what you will' and relates to emotional, spiritual and physical harm. It's important to ask yourself how this applies to whatever you're about to do in your magickal workings and to make sure it's not manipulating anyone's free will or causing a short-term or long-term harmful effect on any living thing. It is perfectly okay to perform spells for selfish needs, as long as it doesn't break this rule. You can be selfish and benefit personally from magickal workings without causing harm to others. It's very important to never carry out magickal workings if you are angry or highly emotional; similarly, you wouldn't perform divination while in a negative or emotionally charged state because your energy would affect the outcome.

Wiccans may follow 'If it harms none, do what you will' as law, but this does not mean that you have to back down in every situation or let people hurt you – and, if people go out of their way to cause you harm, the law doesn't mean that you have to sit back and do nothing, just in case you harm them in some way.

Another factor of this principle is to stop or prevent harm being done. There are two types of wrongdoers; those who do the wrong deed, and those who see the wrong being done and don't try to stop it from happening. If somebody is causing you harm in any way, you have a right to stop this harm. There is always a limit to what you can do, but as long as you follow the law as strictly as you can, remember that balance is the key element here. If harm comes your way, you have a right to put a stop to it. Also, sometimes harming something is inevitable; for example, accidentally, stepping on an insect or accidentally hurting someone's feelings; none of us is perfect and we have to remember this, we are all human beings and everyone makes mistakes.

FREE WILL

Free will is also important to remember during your Wicca practices and magickal workings. Even if you believe that you are doing good and causing no harm to someone during a spell, if you perform a spell that in some way manipulates someone's free will, this is *not* okay. You should never perform a spell that can change someone's actions for your own selfish desires, even if you have the power to do so. For example, if you have a friend who is in a situation with their partner that you feel is bad for them, it is not okay to interfere in this by using a spell to control your friend to make them leave their partner. Even if you feel sure that this is the right decision for your friend, it would be controlling their free will. Always consider whether magickal practices are the correct answer for the situation; there are always several ways to approach a problem. Also, try to put yourself in the other person's situation; ask yourself if you would be okay with this? This doesn't mean that you can't perform spells on other people, just remember not to compromise their free will and consider whether the spell will harm or manipulate them in any way. Some people may not want a spell cast on them even if you are just trying to help! I would suggest asking them before doing anything unless you are certain that they would be happy with your actions.

THE WICCAN REDE

The Wiccan Rede is a set of moral codes or key statements that Wiccans can use as principles to guide their lives. As I said, many, but not all, Wiccans choose to do this. Of course it is entirely a personal choice. The Wiccan Rede is written in the form of a poem and is frequently written at the beginning of your Book of Shadows. The original author of the Wiccan Rede was influenced by several well-known Wiccans dating back many, many years, but in fact the author remains unknown.

The Wiccan Rede

Bide within the Law you must, in perfect Love and perfect Trust.
Live you must and let to live, fairly take and fairly give.

For tread the Circle thrice about to keep unwelcome spirits out.
To bind the spell well every time, let the spell be said in rhyme.

Light of eye and soft of touch, speak you little, listen much.
Honour the Old Ones in deed and name,
let love and light be our guides again.

Deosil go by the waxing moon, chanting out the joyful tune.
Widdershins go when the moon doth wane,
and the werewolf howls by the dread wolfsbane.

When the Lady's moon is new, kiss the hand to Her times two.
When the moon rides at Her peak then your heart's desire seek.

Heed the North winds mighty gale, lock the door and trim the sail.
When the Wind blows from the East, expect the new and set the
feast.

When the wind comes from the South, love will kiss you on the
mouth.
When the wind whispers from the West, all hearts will find peace
and rest.

Nine woods in the Cauldron go, burn them fast and burn them slow.
Birch in the fire goes to represent what the Lady knows.

Oak in the forest towers with might, in the fire it brings the God's
insight. Rowan is a tree of power causing life and magick to flower.

Willows at the waterside stand ready to help us to the Summerland.
Hawthorn is burned to purify and to draw faerie to your eye.

Hazel — the tree of wisdom and learning adds its strength to the
bright fire burning.

White are the flowers of Apple tree that brings us fruits of fertility.
Grapes grow upon the vine giving us both joy and wine.
Fir does mark the evergreen to represent immortality seen.

Elder is the Lady's tree, burn it not or cursed you'll be.
Four times the Major Sabbats mark in the light and in the dark.

As the old year starts to wane the new begins, it's now Samhain.
When the time for Imbolc shows, watch for flowers through the snows.

When the wheel begins to turn soon the Beltane fires will burn.
As the wheel turns to Lamas night power is brought to magick rite.

Four times the Minor Sabbats fall, use the Sun to mark them all.
When the wheel has turned to Yule, light the log the Horned One rules.

In the spring, when night equals day, time for Ostara to come our way.
When the Sun has reached its height, time for Oak and Holly to fight.

Harvesting comes to one and all when the Autumn Equinox does fall.
Heed the flower, bush and tree, by the Lady blessed you'll be.

Where the rippling waters go, cast a stone, the truth you'll know.
When you have and hold a need, harken not to others' greed.

With a fool no season spend or be counted as his friend.
Merry Meet and Merry Part bright the cheeks and warm the heart.

Mind the Three-fold Laws you should, three times bad and three times good.
When misfortune is enow, wear the star upon your brow.

Be true in love, this you must do, unless your love is false to you.

These Eight words the Rede fulfill:

An Ye Harm None, Do What Ye Will.

VEGANISM AND VEGETARIANISM

Another controversial subject which is discussed a great deal in the modern Wiccan world is the question of whether all Wiccans should be vegetarian or vegan. Because many Wiccans live by 'If it harms none, do what you will', this leads to a debate about whether it is acceptable to contribute to harming animals in any way; this includes unnecessary product testing on animals, as well as actually eating animals and animal-related products. Some Wiccans interpret the saying to extend to the earth. Personally, I choose not to eat meat and to only purchase cruelty-free products as far as possible. For me, this relates back to the eight-word saying above, which I try to live by.

However, we have to remember that this choice is not always available to everyone and that others have different priorities and limitations in their lives. As I said before, not everybody thinks and feels the same about things and a Wiccan's choice on how to eat or what to purchase is entirely up to them and we must try to understand one another's differences. Even if we have completely different beliefs, all we can do is discuss with and educate one another on why we feel a certain way, without attacking each other. In my opinion, we should do what we can to prevent harming the earth and other living beings as much as we can; every little thing helps – from making small changes like using cruelty-free make-up and toiletries and maybe having a meat-free day once or twice a week or only consuming meat and/or dairy products at the weekends. It all depends on your own personal ideas about your faith but sometimes, just making a little change or contributing to a more positive, less harmful life by taking tiny steps can have a huge, positive effect on how you engage with the world and how you feel in yourself. This is just something to consider and is not in any way compulsory for being a Wiccan. Veganism and vegetarianism were not major considerations when Wicca was created, but now that we have such easy access to education and discussions on the subject of choosing a low-cruelty lifestyle, these choices seem to be increasingly popular and open for debate in the modern world of Wicca.

5.

Magick

Since the start of my journey in Wicca, I've been asked many questions about magick: What is it? Is it real? Why do you spell it like that? Is it dangerous? There are many misconceptions around magick which have created a fantastical, false idea about what many people think magick is. In reality we do not fly on broomsticks, flick our wands and make frogs appear. Real magick can be numerous things; it can be a ritual, or a spell, it can be the creation of a potion or magick can be divination. Or it can be as simple as cooking a meal for a loved one! Yes, magick is powerful, but there really is nothing to be scared of.

Magick is not imaginary or pretend; we use the power of our five natural senses, combined with the power of nature, crystals, herbs, stones and the five elements (air, fire, water, earth and spirit) to achieve effective results. Magick is everywhere, right in front of us at all times; we put our desire into something and make it happen – this is magick. Numbers, words, colours, thoughts, actions and symbols are all magick, the natural world that surrounds us is magick. A lot of Wiccans believe that everything in our world is made up from the same substance; we are connected to everything else, we are made up from the same matter as the sun, the stars, the earth below us and the sky above us. We are made from the same substance as the entire natural world is made from, presented in a human being. We have the same energies and properties that the earth holds, all within ourselves; we each hold all of the power and energy that we need. If we use our senses to their full potential, we can manipulate energies within nature to gain effective results.

Magick doesn't work by lighting a candle and mixing a few herbs together and saying 'abracadabra', magick comes from within you and your intentions. You can't do spell work without intent; it won't work. There is nothing to be scared of in magick and you should explore it and study it, especially if your intentions are good. However, magick is definitely not easy and it takes *a lot* of practice and adjusting to – and it's extremely draining, as well. Magick also requires getting into the right frame of mind; meditation can help with this as it enables you to tap into your psychic abilities and to open your third eye (heightened intuition and perception). Then maybe after a while you will no longer need to meditate and it will be easier to access.

MAGIC VS MAGICK

Magic with a 'c' is commonly associated with fantasy magic, such as stage tricks; pulling a rabbit out of a hat, etc. It's a form of entertainment and is a performance based on tricks. While magick spelt with a 'k' refers to the type of magick used by witches, Wiccans etc. in witchcraft. Some prefer to use the word 'magick' with a 'k' so that it isn't confused with fantasy magic. You don't have to spell it differently – just be aware that there is a difference between the two.

THE DIFFERENT TYPES OF MAGICK

There are tons of different types of magick, to do with the mediums you use to create or assist it; for example, kitchen magick, herbal magick, candle magick, etc. All of these can be used to cast spells.

SPELLS

Casting spells can take a few different forms, the main two being charming and potions. Spell work is something we do for personal gain and assistance. The energy that you release in spell work will bounce back to stimulate the intent of the spell. A spell could use verbal indications such as chants, sayings or simple word formations, sometimes combined with physical movements and different variations of objects and tools and mediums to create a magickal energy. See the Spell Work chapter in Part 3 (pages 151–66) for starter spells and how to prepare for them.

RITUALS

Many people think that rituals and spells are the same but they are not. Rituals are for a longer lasting purpose; they reach deeper within your core. Rituals are performed as a part of the Wicca faith, you can do them within a group or alone and they are typically used to become closer to the divine.

We usually cast spells for a few main different intentions. Honouring spells can be used specifically for our deities, for the Sabbats or Esbats, or for the deceased. They are used to give thanks to the natural earth, to natural occurrences such as seasons and to your deities (however you perceive them). You can cast a spell to get rid of something, to expel or remove something that you no longer want or need in your life. You can cast spells to bless something or someone – objects or people – and these types of spells can help a situation, a venture or a relationship to begin with good energy and intentions; to create a positive start to something. For example, this type of spell could be used when you or someone you know is moving to a new home; blessing the house will create a positive new beginning. You can also bless new tools that you are going to use in your magickal workings. Existing tools, places and relationships, etc. can also benefit from blessing spells – for instance, maybe you have been going through a period of negativity, for whatever reason, and you feel that this has attached itself to your room, your personal space or haven; blessing the room can create a new energy and new beginning in that area. Or you can cast spells for something that you may want to add to or gain in your life or to help you to create positivity for yourself in some form.

For example, you might be hoping for a promotion at work and you can cast a spell to help with this.

POTIONS

A potion is a mixture of ingredients that, when combined in the proper fashion, has magickal energy. A potion can be a blend of herbs, oils, teas or other natural materials. Potions can be used externally, bathed in, or consumed by drinking or eating, sometimes even steaming, or burning. Potions are so diverse; there is probably a potion for every type of spell that you may need! There is no specific potion or spell for each subject and intent; for example, there is no one potion for a love spell. There are lots of different ones and every combination works differently on every person. Liquid potions should be stored in bottles, jars are best for dried materials or, if the potion is not suitable for storing, be sure to discard it properly, by burying it in the ground, for example.

WHEN IS THE BEST TIME TO DO MAGICK?

There are certain times of the month, week and moon phases that are the optimum times for particular magick or to ask for specific things. We follow the moon during magick. The moon is our goddess and has a huge impact on our earth and has associations with everything that grows and is created. It enhances psychic knowledge.

WAXING MOON

The waxing moon is the time straight after the new moon, when the goddess in is her maiden form. This is a beneficial time to do spells for growth, new comings, also improving things, any aspect of your life that may need this, such as career, love life, friendships and spiritually. This is a time for increasing aspects of your life. It's also a great time for magick that's connected with changes, taking up new hobbies, financial spells and balance spells too.

WANING MOON

From after the full moon to until it's the new moon again is the phase of the waning moon. This is a good time for banishing spells, removing obstacles and health and wellness spells, for both mental and physical well-being. This is also a great time to decrease the negative aspects of our lives, to get rid of or 'lessen' anything that we feel we need to. Also, it is a time to let go of any-thing affecting your happiness, whether it be any angry thoughts and feelings you may have towards someone or situations causing you stress or rage. Spells for clarity and to help you understand the way to move forwards in a situation, and cleansing spells are also relevant at this time too. The goddess is in her wise crone form in this phase.

NEW MOON

The new moon is always the best time for spell work relating to new beginnings and ventures, in any form, whether it be looking for new love, a new job or starting on a new path or phase in our lives. It's also good for beginning to let go of the past and starting afresh. It's a beneficial phase in which to assess what is required to change in our lives in order for them to progress and grow. Change is good – we need it to remove what no longer serves us, to remove anything that has a negative impact in our lives. The new moon is a fantastic time to look to the future. The triple moon goddess is in a secretive state and the moon is dark.

FULL MOON

In Wicca, the celebration of a full moon is called an Esbat, (see Part 3, Wiccan Holidays and the Wheel of the Year for Esbats and how to celebrate them). This is a relevant time for numerous types of magick, as the night of the full moon is the most magickal night of each month. It's a good time for magick related to healing, strength, power, money, dreams and psychic knowledge. It's an excellent time of the month to draw the energy from the moon to help create positive energy within yourself and your life and to bring about bigger changes. It is generally a good time for 'bigger' spells, where you require more energy and power. It's a beneficial time to meditate on important issues in order to find answers, and divination is also at its most powerful. Psychic energy is radiating from the moon now and it's also time to use that to its full potential for significant and powerful magick. The goddess is in her motherly form at the full moon.

MAGICK ACCORDING TO THE DAYS OF THE WEEK

MONDAY

Monday is named after the moon, and associated with moon deities.
Colour correspondences: Silver, white and blue.
Magickal intent for Monday: discovering unknown knowledge, uncovering mystery, illusion, sleep, emotions, travels, peace, fertility, insight, creativity, wisdom, new starts, dreams and seeking answers.

TUESDAY

Tuesday is associated with the planet Mars.
Colour correspondences: Red and orange.
Magickal intent for Tuesday: Conflict/resolving conflict, success, overcoming obstacles, protection, cleansing and strength.

WEDNESDAY

Wednesday is associated with Mercury.
Colour correspondences: Purple, lavender and orange.
Magickal intent for Wednesday: finance, change, creativity, work, luck, improvement and art.

THURSDAY

Thursday is associated with Jupiter.
Colour correspondences: blue, green and purple.
Magickal intent for Thursday: strength, protection, overpowering obstacles, healing, inner strength, mental health and physical health.

FRIDAY

Friday is associated with Venus.
Colour correspondences: pink, red and light blue.
Magickal intent for Friday: fertility, love, relationships, friendships, sex, passion, birth, romance and improvement.

SATURDAY

Saturday is associated with Saturn.
Colour correspondences: black, purple and deep red.
Magickal intent for Saturday: wisdom, psychic abilities, protection, banishing, safety and cleansing.

SUNDAY

Sunday is associated with the sun.
Colour correspondences: yellow and gold.
Magickal intent for Sunday: peace, self-expression, creativity, fame, promotion, career, wealth, healing, growth and victory.

IS THERE A WRONG TIME TO DO MAGICK?

There are so many good opportunities to do magick, but unfortunately, sometimes, there are times when it just shouldn't be used or it just isn't the appropriate time. Magick should only be performed when you are feeling at your neutral mental state, no matter what that might be (it is different for every individual). You don't have to be ecstatically happy or extremely positive, just in the clearest, most reasonable mental state that you can be in. Being angry or creating a spell out of anger is never good; it can reflect in your magick and come back to you. It is the same with being highly emotional, sad or overly stressed. Also, doing a spell from the perspective of purely seeking revenge or in order to harm someone is never good. Always look to the law of three (or Three-Fold Law) if you're undecided over whether to do something or not and, if you're not sure, meditate on it, seek the answer and then rethink. If you're just not feeling up to doing a magickal working that you have planned, for whatever reason, there will always be an opportunity to do it at another time, so there's no need to rush, it will work a lot more effectively when you're feeling up to it.

RULES OF MAGICK

There are a few rules that *some* (but not all) Wiccans like to follow when casting their magick to ensure that they are following the law of three.

☾ If you can solve the situation without magick, do so. Magick is not used to solve something that you simply can't be bothered to sort out in other ways; that lack of thought and energy will show in your magick and the outcome will be unsuccessful. For example, if you're having problems with someone that you cannot avoid – a co-worker or someone who attends the same classes as you but who is manipulative, a bully or who generally brings harmful energies – try to think of ways to confront them, involve other people to help you or physically distance yourself from them. Explore all other avenues before turning to magick. This might solve the problem, but even if it doesn't, you will have the motivation for magick, which will make its use far more successful.

ℭ As we spoke about in the chapter on Three-Fold Law (see pages 26–33), never manipulate free will while casting spells.

ℭ Remember 'If it harms none, do what you will' – a line from the Wiccan Rede (see pages 30–1) which some Wiccans try to always follow.

ℭ Don't be greedy, Wicca is all about balance; don't ask for the world. For example, you may want to improve your career, so, instead of asking to instantly become the CEO of the company that you're working for, you could do a spell to help boost some aspects of your career and to help you advance along your chosen path. It's always important to be aware of maintaining balance, because whatever you're asking for has to come from somewhere; materialistic things don't just appear. This doesn't necessarily mean that you *can't* ask for something big if it's in great need; just make sure that you balance it out. In order to gain something, maybe you could sacrifice something else; for example, perhaps you need a promotion, but maybe some of the money you get once you've been promoted could go to charity to help someone else, or you could use your position to assist somebody in need in your line of work.

6.

Wiccan Paths

Unlike some religions, Wicca is adaptable to you, your lifestyle and who you are as a person. Of course, there are basic principles and beliefs, such as the fundamental 'If it harms none, do what you will' and the eight Sabbats and twelve Esbats which are celebrated by all Wiccans. There are also, unfortunately, people in the Wiccan community that think their way of practising is the only correct way. However, I have also found that there are crazy amounts of paths or traditions you can follow to make the amazing journey that you are embarking on right for you. Basically, Wicca is adaptable for anyone who has a passion for the faith.

WHY WOULD YOU CHOOSE ONE WICCA PATH OVER ANOTHER?

All humans are unique: we each have different desires, feelings, beliefs and powers in us, and if some traditions and paths may suit one person, they might not make sense to another. Choosing a Wicca path that feels right for you can also help you find your way in the faith; the basis of your chosen path, its magickal workings and practices, can provide you with a much clearer route for your Wiccan journey. The path that you follow can also help to shape your identity as a Wiccan – which can be both personal and important to the individual.

FINDING YOUR PATH

So, how do you decide which path is right for you? It's actually a lot easier than it sounds. Typically, in order to find your Wiccan identity, you can research into the different traditions and paths until you find one that suits your beliefs and interests or that you simply feel drawn to on some level. You might find that you are already instinctively following some of the traditions that relate to a particular path. Some people like to use divination to determine which route to take while others just seem to know instinctively! Many Wiccans, myself included, may feel that they identify with more than one path, for example, I'm an eclectic Wiccan, but I also practise the faith independently, without a coven, so I'm an eclectic solitary Wiccan (see the following sections for further explanation of what I mean). You can combine paths that work together if it feels right for you to do so. There are no restrictions or rules about how you decide which path is best for you. I have described a list of Wicca paths and traditions that I feel can help you make an informed choice. Also, remember that people change paths all the time, you can follow many different traditions in a lifetime and some paths may suit you at certain points in your life and at other times you may feel a different path works better for you.

I am going to explain a little about some of the different types of Wicca paths and traditions that you can follow. First, I would like to say that this is not a definitive list, but it includes the main paths that I am aware of and am educated about. If none of these feel right for you, there are still lots of others and, as I said, it's completely fine to combine paths as I have. There are some limitations in that some traditions don't work together, but, in Wicca, I don't feel there are many restrictions or limitations on what you can do. So, it is about thinking over which path is best for you in the faith to help you with your journey and guidance. This is just a short list of the traditions in Wicca that you can follow and a short briefing on them, so please do some of your own research online and in the many reference books available. Also please remember that each path is open to individual interpretation and may mean different things to different practitioners. I hope this section helps you with deciding your own correct Wicca path.

DIFFERENT TYPES OF WICCA PATHS

GARDNERIAN WICCA

I'm starting with this very well-known Wicca path. Gardnerian Wicca was created by Gerald Gardner, who is considered to be pretty much like the dad of Wicca. Around the middle of the twentieth century, Gardner had a huge influence on the Wicca faith; he was responsible for promoting the religion throughout the world. The Gardnerian path is a coven-based path which supposedly follows insight and practices that Gardner learned from his previous experiences with other groups. In the Gardnerian path, you typically only follow one god and one goddess. It is believed that Gardnerian coven practices are kept secret from anyone not initiated, that Gardnerian Wiccans cannot share the fact they are in a coven and that they have to sign an oath to keep the secrets of the coven safe. This might be why there is a lack of published information about the actual Gardnerian beliefs and practices. Gardner has initiated many High Priestesses and High Priests to lead their own covens and membership is only achieved through initiation by these High Priestesses or High Priests. There is thought to be a system of hierarchy or levels attained within this path. It follows that it is rare to find a solitary Wiccan practising this path.

CELTIC WICCA

Celtic Wicca is a more modern form of Wicca. Its traditions teach a deep-rooted love for the earth and spirituality and it incorporates Celtic lore. The Celtic path typically has two main deities:

the Mother Earth Goddess and the Horned God but can also have other minor deities that they can still worship and help with their practices which are typically from a Celtic/druid pantheon. They study the magickal properties of plants and crystals, stones, herbs, flowers, trees, elemental spirits, gnomes, sprites and fairies, which they also use heavily in their magickal workings, including rituals and spell work. Celtic Wicca can be learned and practised solitarily but some practitioners of Celtic Wicca believe that being part of a druid-led coven helps the followers of this path find their way.

ALEXANDRIAN WICCA

Alexandrian Wicca was introduced by Alex Sanders in the 1960s. It is heavily influenced by Gardnerian Wicca, being coven-based, with rituals led by a High Priest and Priestess, and members who are initiated have to sign an oath of secrecy to the coven. The differences between Alexandrian and Gardnerian paths are firstly the deities; instead of believing in two principal deities as Gardner teaches, in this path you can believe in any number of deities and from whichever pantheon you please. Sanders had practised Gardnerian Wicca throughout his life and felt as though it was too controlled and forced. This particular path incorporates elements of ceremonial magick and Qabalah. Alexandrian wiccans are thought to emphasise gender polarity; I feel that it is a good thing that this emphasis is decreasing in the modern world of Wicca as we learn more, progress and grow as a community.

ECLECTIC WICCA

Eclectic Wicca is one of the paths with the greatest following. As I mentioned previously, I identify as an eclectic Wiccan. An eclectic Wiccan does not follow a specific tradition but picks and chooses specific deities that they are drawn to; for instance, they could follow any sets of deities or can just pick and choose one or any number from different paths. Some eclectic Wiccans believe that all the deities represent the same entities but they just stem from different cultures and are presented in different ways. The majority of eclectic Wiccans are solitary Wiccans but there are, of course, a lot of covens that have eclectic Wiccans, as it's a very accessible path for your Wicca journey.

SHAMAN WICCA

For an extremely long time, Shaman practice was seen as an individual path, distinct from Wicca. Nowadays, being a Shaman and a Wicca are thought of as being a very modern combination despite the fact that uniting the two paths has been a tradition for longer than we could imagine. Shaman Wiccans follow the same typical traditions as other Wiccans but they use their practices and techniques to connect with the spirit/sacred realms. Shaman Wiccans can reach different states of consciousness, speak to spirits from which they gain knowledge and answers and predict the future. Shamans also practise both physical and spiritual healing. A Shaman Wiccan can follow any deities they would like but can also use spirits to help with magickal workings. Again, Shamans can be solitary or work within a group or coven.

SEAX WICCA

Seax Wicca is heavily influenced by the folklore of Anglo-Saxon traditions. It was founded by Raymond Buckland, who was originally a Gardnerian Wiccan who moved from England to the United States in the 1970s, where he created this new path. Buckland established a more accessible and open path in that Seax Wiccan covens follow a democratic system, electing officers and High Priests and Priestesses with a yearly vote. There is also no secret oath taken. Runes play a significant part in divinatory practices. You can follow this path solitarily but because of its openness, joining a coven or an online coven may be a good path to take if this suits your life-style. There is no one set of rules or regulations for Seax Wicca.

DIANIC WICCA

Dianic Wicca is a feminist form of Wicca that is quickly growing in popularity. This path was founded by a hereditary witch named Zsuzsanna Budapest, in 1971, in Venice Beach, California. This path generally follows the typical traditions of Gardnerian and Alexandrian Wicca. However, Dianic Wiccans tend to focus on female energies and the goddess side of things and not so much on the god and male energy side of things. They also focus on female deities but typically worship one main deity, which is the Roman hunter goddess Diana. Typically, this path is for females only and works to create a safe space for women who may not, for various reasons, feel comfortable practising with men.

HEREDITARY WICCA

Hereditary Wicca is the term for a Wiccan that is born into a family that also practises the Wicca faith or has ancestors that have practised Wicca, even if they follow a different path to their family. A Hereditary Wiccan may be brought up as a Wiccan or they might decide to adopt the Wiccan faith into their lives later on but, either way, they come from a family that practises it. Once again, Hereditary Wicca can be combined with other paths. Hereditary Wiccans can sometimes be part of a family coven or choose to practise as a solitary Wiccan.

SOLITARY WICCA

As you could probably guess from the name, a solitary Wiccan does not belong to any coven or group and mainly practises the faith alone. As with eclectic Wicca, solitary Wiccans follow whichever deities they are drawn to, and they are not limited to a specific number of deities; they may follow just one or a whole pantheon. Today, many Wiccans choose to be solitary because they want to explore a path or multiple paths and make their own discoveries in the faith. If you define yourself as solitary, you are probably not actively looking to join a group or coven.

FAERY WICCA

A Faery Wiccan places importance on the fae; sprites, faeries, elves, gnomes, etc. who keep everything balanced in the natural world. Faery Wicca developed from early Celtic traditions and beliefs. Faery Wiccans tend to practise faery magick and work closely with faeries and other members of the fae. They also use faery power, an energy from the fae. They work with faery energies and hold them in high regard, above other deities. Some believe that Faery Wiccans should only worship the fae themselves as their deities whilst others worship an eclectic mix of deities, depending on individual preference. Some people in the Faery Wicca community also like to have specific Wiccan names for themselves (this is common with other traditions as well).

DRACONIC WICCA

Draconic Wiccans worship dragons and dragon lore. Believe it or not, dragons and dragon lore are part of the super ancient beliefs and customs of many different cultures. Draconic Wiccans mainly practise Draconian magick, which is powered by the strong energies of dragons. For most practitioners of Draconic Wicca, dragons represent wisdom and balance. It is common for them to work with dragon gods and goddesses, who are called to you or into you in times when needed the most – Sabbats, during a full moon or if you have a powerful spell to tackle. They also call on elemental dragon guardians for rituals which represent the elements used in traditional Wicca practices. Draconic Wiccans, again, can be in a coven or clan or practise solitarily. Draconic Wicca practices are usually passed down by word of mouth but as this path increases in popularity, more published information is becoming available if you would like to do further research.

GREEN WICCAN

A Green Wiccan practises mainly nature-based and earth-oriented witchcraft. They typically use herbs, flowers, trees, fungi and plants in kitchen magick (which can be a separate Wicca path in itself) and herbology. Also, growing their own gives them a deeper connection to the plants. Green Wiccans usually practise witchcraft using elements of the earth, rocks, crystals and fossils. Green witches also tend to specialise in herbal remedies. Green Wiccans can follow whichever deities they choose or they might specifically follow nature spirits, which are the dead of humans, animals and plants. A form of green witchcraft which is better classified as Green Wicca was popularised by Ann Moura. This connects to the forest, but places a lot of emphasis on folklore and folk magick from a wide range of cultures. Green Wiccans can be solitary practitioners or part of a coven. Many Wiccans follow some of the Green Wicca practices, particularly growing their own herbs for use in their practices.

AFRO-WICCA

Afro-Wiccans follow the Wheel of the Year, celebrating and honouring the natural world. They perform rituals and spell work according to the sun and the moon and follow the Wiccan Rede and the law of three, and live by the rule 'If it harms none, do what you will'. Followers of Afro-Wicca will invoke, honour and worship deities from the Egyptian, African and Afro-Caribbean pantheons. Their magickal workings might include practices found in rootwork, voodoo and hoodoo. Afro-Wicca is a relatively new path of eclectic Wicca; it is a combination of paths in which some practitioners include elements of their cultural heritage and energies while still following the main beliefs and practices of the Wicca faith.

DECIDING ON PRACTISING SOLITARILY OR IN A COVEN?

Deciding on whether you want to practise solitarily or in a coven can be super easy and lots of factors can determine what's best for you. Like I said before, there may be a path you are drawn to that is coven-based, while some other paths can be more flexible and can be practised in a coven or solitarily.

Some people feel their level of concentration and power within the world is best alone, and some feel it increases when they are surrounded by people sharing the same path as them.

Either way, there are positives to being in a coven, like learning from other incredible Wiccans all embarking on the same path as you, having a community to share your journey and the Wicca path with, including the Sabbats and spell and ritual work, and also having a group of people to be a part of spiritually – which can also include amazing support.

You can look into joining an online coven or search for one that you can be a part of in the real world. You could find that you enjoy being in a community with like-minded people and accept that you're going to be learning from other Wiccans and taught a specific way for the path you have chosen. Find out more on how to find your coven on pages 220–3.

On the other hand, you may like to practise the faith alone, and embark on your journey alone because you may feel you can concentrate and strive within your magickal workings and that being solitary may give you the freedom to create your own journey and possibly a broader path. Practising the faith solitarily can give you an opportunity to do things your way, and make your path your own.

For most Wiccans, it's completely normal to fall naturally into being in a coven or to practise the faith on their own. Whichever path you choose, though, whether solitary or a coven, you can always change your way.

A Wiccan's will is free.

7.

The Book of Shadows

A Book of Shadows is a personal record that anyone embarking on a Wicca journey can use to document absolutely everything that they learn and discover along the way. It is your own book that can be used to record your personal and individual growth in the faith. You might include spells, rituals, potions, aspects of magick, chants, information on the elements, magickal tools used in your workings, divination such as information gathered from tarot cards, tasseography, rune stones, etc. You also might include more personal information, such as your own deities, your path, information about your own particular magick tools and documentation of individual methods and results of your spell and ritual work. It is important to keep documentation of all your work as a Wiccan – for me, the main reason is that a Book of Shadows holds so much information about your personal Wicca journey which can be looked back on and reflected on at a later date.

A Book of Shadows can be any type of book, but it is preferable to begin with a durable, thick book because, trust me, there will be a hell of a lot of information to fill it with. It can be hardback or paperback and some people like to use binders and loose pages because they are easy to arrange, add to and put neatly in order – all super helpful for documenting your journey. Also, an ordered Book of Shadows can make it easier when you need to look back at a particular section or subject. Some Wiccans choose to have one book documenting everything; others work on multiple Books of Shadows. Personally, I find that it works well for me to have two books; one for recording practical experiences, such as spell work, and one that I use more for recording information, such as the historical side of spells and why I might use them. It is entirely up to you: start recording your journey and see what feels right and makes sense.

However many Books of Shadows you start with, the chances are that you will end up having more than one in your lifetime. You will find that you never stop learning and recording, so after you've finished your first Book of Shadows, simply purchase or make another and continue the documentation of your Wicca journey.

A Book of Shadows is like any of our magickal tools that we keep safe and sacred to us. Many Wiccans find that they prefer to keep their books extremely private, because they are so very personal – similar to keeping a journal. It is absolutely fine if you feel that you don't want anyone to see your book. Alternatively, some Wiccans are more open and not so protective, allowing close family and friends and people they trust access to their books. Once again, everyone feels differently and it is up to the individual to decide their level of privacy.

WHAT IS THE DIFFERENCE BETWEEN A BOOK OF SHADOWS AND A GRIMOIRE?

While a Book of Shadows is a record of your own personal exper-iences as already described, a Grimoire is similar but would not include personal paths and choices, such as your own personal deities, information on how you do your own spells or your own individual methods. It focuses on the practical and factual elements of your journey. Families and covens are likely to have a Grimoire to share their teachings with the entire group and they also may have a Book of Shadows. A Grimoire is not usually written for one specific Wiccan. You will find that the way you document your journey will naturally fall into the style of a Book of Shadows or a Grimoire.

CREATING YOUR OWN BOOK OF SHADOWS

There are lots and lots of commercially produced Books of Shadows these days that have been designed and printed worldwide, but I strongly recommend creating and writing your own. I believe that documenting your own growth and achievements helps you learn and progress on your path and helps you to discover your own identity and to become the Wiccan you would like to be. Starting your Book of Shadows can be really confusing and nerve-wracking, but remember there's no rush; you have the rest of your life to write about your newfound faith.

One of the most difficult parts (for me anyway) of creating your Book of Shadows is actually getting started. You can begin by personalising the cover of your book to suit your Wicca journey and yourself. Some choose to leave this until later, when they know how they'd like to express themselves – perhaps decorating it to suit a path they have chosen or aspects of the faith that they would like to emphasise or reflect. Some leave it blank or decorate it simply with a pentagram. The possibilities are endless. Here are some ideas to help kick-start your journey – but really just follow your heart.

- Symbols that are relevant to your journey, for example, pentagrams, pentacles, protection symbols, element symbols, god and goddess symbolism, etc.
- Crystals (preferably ones that are relevant to you, ones for spiritual protection or that you are drawn to)
- Relevant or interesting drawings, paintings, pictures
- Make or buy a cover for it
- Dried herbs or flowers (make sure to glue these down well)
- Feathers, shells or other natural objects
- Protection charms, written normally or in code
- Lace or string for decoration or protection

And now some ideas to get you started with documentation in your Book of Shadows:

- A protection charm
- The Wiccan Rede – or any other moral codes you may follow
- Deities you work with and connect with
- Notes about a path or tradition you may have chosen to follow (for now) for your Wicca journey
- Elements
- The Sabbats and Esbats
- Divination information
- Dreams and interpretations
- Ritual work
- Spell work
- Potions
- Herbs, flowers and their properties
- Different types of Magick you learn about
- Chants
- Information on magickal tools
- Magickal workings and your way of doing things

After you have taken those first steps in creating and writing your Book of Shadows, you will enjoy building a relationship with your book as you record more and more, whether it is in the form of notes, drawings, found objects, clippings, artwork or anything else that you choose to include.

8.

Deities

In Wicca, the deities are gods or goddesses that we follow and worship. There are so many deities that you could follow and many ways that you can choose to see and worship them. There are no right or wrong choices here. It simply depends on what feels right to you – which deities you feel drawn to and also the path that you decide to take as a Wiccan.

Do not be put off Wicca because the idea of having a god or a goddess doesn't feel like your thing. Following deities is actually very simple. A lot of Wiccans don't think of gods and goddesses as actual people, higher beings, someone that once existed or as all-knowing creators of everything. Instead, we view deities as personifications of nature. Each deity represents a different aspect of something that we experience on this earth, including the natural world; there is a god or a goddess to represent every single aspect of the earth and all that comes with it. It becomes easier to connect with nature if we see aspects of it in human form, because we find it easier to understand and visualise looking up to, listening to and communicating with people. So, we see deities as just human forms of nature. For example, the Armenian deity Anahit is the goddess of fertility, healing, wisdom and water, and we think of her as the personification of these elements and powers and the spiritual energies surrounding them. Of course, you can also believe in deities in the traditional way, as supernatural powers that keep whatever they represent and look after in balance; that's just another way of believing in your deities.

Some Wiccans might follow a group or pantheon of deities such as the Celtic, Norse or Egyptian gods and goddesses. It's also a common idea that gods and goddesses from different pantheons represent similar things, so they are actually similar deities that have originated from and developed and adapted in different civilisations and cultures throughout the world. If you believe this train of thought and you are happy to potentially honour all of the deities, depending on which feels right for you at the time, you could be an eclectic Wiccan. Or you could just choose one group of deities to work with if you prefer and still follow this belief, but just choose one pantheon that suits you best and you feel drawn to. Some Wiccans only worship one or two deities and others may just choose to work with one god or goddess if the pull towards that one deity seems sufficient. Some Wiccans follow the traditional Gardnerian teaching, believing there is only one god and one goddess – the god of the sun and the goddess of the moon. There are so many deities that you can follow from different cultures and countries. Don't worry if it takes you a while to find which gods and goddesses feel right for you. You can worship deities from anywhere in the world, but there are a few common ones that you hear about frequently in Wicca. This doesn't mean that you have to follow these ones, these are just a few of the options.

GREEK

Apollo – god of music, prophecy, truth, healing, the sun and
   light
Aphrodite – goddess of love, beauty, eternal youth and fertility
Ares – god of war
Artemis – goddess of the hunt, wild animals, chastity and
   childbirth
Asteria – goddess of falling stars and night-time prophecies
Athena – goddess of wisdom, strength, crafts and knowledge

Aura – goddess representing a gentle breeze
Demeter – goddess of the harvest
Eos – goddess of the dawn
Eros – god of love
Hecate – goddess of magick, witchcraft, ghosts and the night
Hades – god of the underworld
Helios – god of the sun
Hera – goddess of women, marriage and family
Hermes – god of trade, shepherds, travel and literature, particularly of poets, also the messenger of the gods
Nyx – goddess of the night
Persephone – goddess of the spring and queen of the underworld
Poseidon – god of the sea, earthquakes, floods and horses
Rhea – mother of gods and goddess of motherhood and female fertility
Selene – goddess of the moon
Styx – goddess of the river Styx which divides earth from the underworld
Thea – goddess of sight and divine light
Zeus – the god of the sky and the ruler of the Olympian gods.

ROMAN

Apollo – god of light, music and healing
Aurora – goddess of the dawn
Bacchus – god of wine, farming and fertility
Ceres – goddess of the harvest and a mother's love
Cupid – god of love
Diana – goddess of the hunt, nature and the moon
Juno – goddess of love and marriage

Jupiter – god of thunder and sky
Luna – goddess of the moon
Mars – god of war
Minerva – goddess of wisdom, war, commerce, crafts and
    poetry
Neptune – god of the sea
Pluto – god of the underworld
Proserpine – goddess of the underworld
Sol – god of the sun
Terra – goddess of the earth
Venus – goddess of love

EGYPTIAN

Amun – god of the sun, the air and life
Anubis – god of the dead
Bast – goddess of protection, cats and of the home
Bes – god of war, but also of the home
Hapi – god of water and fertility who brought the annual
    flooding of the Nile
Hathor – goddess of joy, love, motherhood, beauty and
    fertility
Horus – protector of Egypt
Isis – goddess of fertility and empowerment
Khensu – god of the moon
Maat – goddess of truth, justice, stability and harmony
Min – god of fertility and male sexuality
Mut – goddess, mother figure
Neith – goddess of war
Nut – goddess of the sky and the heavens
Osiris – god of the afterlife
Ptah – god of craftsmen and creation

Ra – god of the sun
Sekhmet – goddess of destruction, war and healing
Set – god of disorder, storms and war
Shu – god of dry air and the earth's atmosphere
Taweret – goddess of childbirth
Tefnut – goddess of water, moisture and rain
Thoth – god of writing, science, magick and the moon

CELTIC

Áine of Knockainey – goddess of love, crops and farms
Airmid – goddess of medicinal plants and regeneration
Amaethon – god of agriculture and luck
Andraste – goddess of the moon and divination
Angus Og – god of youth, beauty and love
Anu – goddess of the moon, fertility, prosperity and comfort
Arawn – god of the underworld, revenge, war and terror
Artio – goddess of animals and fertility
Bel – god representing sun and fire
Bendigeidfran – god of the arts, music, writing and
     prophecy
Branwen – goddess of love and beauty
Bres – god of agriculture and fertility
Brigit/ Brigid – goddess of fire, sun, hearth, fertility, crafts,
     inspiration, home and divination
Cailleach – goddess of the winter months
Ceridwen – goddess of poetic inspiration
Cernunnos – the horned god of nature, the underworld,
     wealth and physical love and masculine energy
The Dagda – god of protection, weather and knowledge and
     the father god of Ireland
Danu – goddess of water, wizards, magick and wisdom

Latobius – god of mountains and sky
Lugh – god of craftsmanship and light
Manannan – god of the sea
Maponus – god of music and poetry
Morrigan – goddess of war
Nuada – god of war
Rhiannon – goddess of horses
Taliesin – god of poets
Taranis – god of thunder and the wheel

NORSE

Aegir – god of the sea
Balder – a gentle, pure and wise god
Bragi – god of poetry and eloquence
Eir – goddess of healing
Forseti – god of justice
Freyja – goddess of fertility, beauty and war
Frigg – goddess of love, fertility and motherhood
Gefion – goddess of fertility
Heimdall – god of light
Hel – ruler of the underworld
Lofn – goddess of marriages
Loki – the trickster of the Norse gods
Njord – god of the wind and sea
Odin – king of the Norse gods; god of poetry, war, death
    and wisdom
Sif – goddess of fertility
Sjöfn – goddess of passion
Skadi – goddess of winter, the hunt and mountains
Thor – god of thunder
Ullr – god of archery and skiing

Var – goddess of marriage oaths
Vör – goddess who knows everything

SLAVIC

Dažbog – god of the sun
Jarilo – god of war, spring, fertility and harvest
Lada – goddess of love, marriage, summer, beauty and
    fertility
Morana – goddess of harvest, winter, death and witchcraft
Perun – god of thunder and lightning
Rod – the supreme god
Svarog – god of fire
Svetovid – god of war and fertility
Triglav – god of war
Veles – god of earth, forests, waters and the underworld
Vesna – goddess of spring, love and youth
Zaria – goddess of beauty
Živa – goddess of love and fertility

JAPANESE

Amaterasu – goddess of the sun and the universe
Benzaiten – goddess of literature, music, love and wealth
Ebisu – god of fishermen, luck, prosperity and crops
Fujin – god of the wind
Inari – goddess of prosperity, fertility, rice, tea, sake,
    agriculture and industry

Jizo – the guardian of children, childbirth, women and
   travellers
Kannon – goddess of mercy
Raijin – god of lightening, storms and thunder

AFRICAN

Anayaroli – god of harvest and wealth (the Temne of Sierra
   Leone)
Asa – god of protection and mercy (the Kamba of Kenya)
Asase Yaa – goddess of fertility (the Ashanti of West Africa)
Chiuta – god of rain (the Tumbuka in Malawi)
Inanna – goddess of sky, war and love (the Banyarwanda)
Jok – god of rain (Zaire and Uganda)
Mungo – god of rain (Giriama of Kenya)
Ngami – goddess of the moon
Ochumare – goddess of rainbows (the Yoruba)
Ogun – god of war and iron (the Nago and the Yoruba)
Olorun – creator god (the Yoruba)
Oshun – the goddess of love and fertility (the Yoruba)
Oya – goddess of storms (the Yoruba)
Rock-Sens – god of weather (the Serer of Gambia)
Ruhanga – creator god and god of fertility, disease and death
   (the Banyoro of Uganda)
Shango – god of thunder, war and magick (the Yoruba)
Yemaya – goddess of the seas and rivers (the Yoruba)
Yemoja – goddess of the river, women and children
   (the Yoruba)

Part
2

Why Explore Wicca?

Wicca has had such a positive impact on all areas of my life. So many elements of the faith go hand in hand with improved physical and mental well-being and positive emotional health and relationships.

9.

Mental Health Benefits

Thankfully, mental health issues are recognised and discussed much more openly nowadays. A question that I am frequently asked is, can I still be a Wiccan if I have a mental health issue?

My answer is always the same. Yes, of course you can. There are so many different mental health issues that people struggle with daily. You can work alongside them to develop your Wicca journey, hopefully improving or at least helping your mental health. It's always important to bear in mind that when you are feeling highly emotional or just not okay, it's fine to take time for yourself. Don't perform spell work or rituals when you're not feeling up to it. Always consider the law of three, if you're in two minds about doing magick, and make sure you are in a neutral state. It doesn't make you a lesser Wiccan if you don't feel up to doing your tarot cards one day or celebrating a Sabbat. Wicca is a lifelong journey and if you intend to be in it for the long run, there's always another time – everything happens in a cycle.

Having a Wicca journey can create something to focus on, to distract your mind – giving you something to look forward to and discover each day. This can be a huge benefit while struggling with mental health issues. Even when the world feels like a difficult, flat place, Wicca helps you look into the natural beauty of it all, making you realise that, no, this isn't 'it': there is more.

I also feel that Wicca encourages you to go outside and experience the natural world. The fundamentals of the faith do not need the day-to-day things we are distracted by. It helps you take a look around, notice plants, trees, the stars, the moon and the sun, aspects of the world you may not always take notice of. It can help you see how beautiful the world is, even when that seems to disappear when you are struggling. Not to mention, there are lots of aspects of Wicca that involve mental, physical and spiritual healing, which can help to balance your mind and emotions. Healing with crystals, herbal remedies, healing using spells and also, the most important, meditation.

Meditation can help numerous aspects of your life: everyday life can offer so much stress, especially when dealing with mental health issues.

Things that can hit people without mental health issues hard can hit those *with* them harder. Meditation helps you escape; it makes you see the world from a bird's-eye view and your problems appear minuscule sometimes or, at least, more manageable. It helps balance your mind and body, relaxes every sense and taps into the parts of your brain that are subconscious to help your mind work through problems you may not be able to deal with on a day-to-day basis. It can help you make the correct decisions and lead your mind to what you truly want, which will inevitably benefit you.

Wicca can benefit the way you think, feel and allow you to experience beautiful aspects of the world, but it is not a cure. We require help from all around us. Remember what we said about science? It's all magick. There's nothing wrong with not being able to cure your mental illness with meditation and healthy eating alone: sometimes you require help from the magick of science and medication – and that's totally okay.

CONFIDENCE

As well as being a factor that can contribute to your mental health, Wicca can also help you gain confidence, which, in turn, can benefit your mental health too. Early on in my Wicca journey, I noticed that my faith helped me create an identity, not based on how everyone else sees me, but on how I see myself. Discovering aspects of Wicca, such as which path suits you best, the deities you feel attracted to, crystals you feel a connection with, tools you use that really do 'choose you', can make you feel as though you are a part of something larger – they did me. Wicca makes you feel as though there is a place for everyone.

Should you keep your beliefs private or talk about them? Sometimes exploring other Wiccans' journeys can be amazing and also contribute to your knowledge and this may require talking to people. Your confidence may be lacking, especially when it comes to talking to people, but finding a place and starting a journey can give you a common ground with other Wiccans. You may want to go to events for your new faith, take part in forums and download apps that help you connect with fellow Wiccans. Your curiosity and ambition to learn in the faith can push you to *want* to speak to others following similar paths to you. Confidence can also be gained in places that you might never have imagined, such as performing magick. This can be a physical task that sometimes takes action, speaking, asking and requesting from the universe, which require massive amounts of power and intent. The actual performance aspect of spell work and rituals can build your confidence, kind of like practising a performance before you go on stage in a play. Magick can also give you a massive sense of self-empowerment; having control over aspects of your life you may not have felt before can build up the confidence inside you to create change, which a lot of young boys and girls struggle with in the modern world. Becoming power-hungry can be a problem, though, so remember to keep humble and balanced throughout your practices. Balance can also help you gain confidence, accepting that everything is as it is: nobody is better than anyone else, no one is worse off, we are all at balance with each other, we do not need to be in competition with each other because we are all individual people – just because someone may be skinnier than you or have more Instagram followers, that doesn't make them better than you. You are just as relevant and as powerful as they are, the earth will serve you the same as it will them. The world is a gift to appreciate; without it, there would be nothing, no life, no people. None of the superficial and fake aspects of the world would matter. We are all one. All of us are original, yet we are all made from the same thing.

MY EXPERIENCE WITH MENTAL HEALTH AND WICCA

Like a lot of people, I have struggled with my own mental health issues. While these were ongoing, I discovered witchcraft. I had times where I felt I didn't physically have the power I needed to perform magick, but I always came back to it. It took me a while to discover magick will always be there; it's not going anywhere. During my recovery, I discovered Wicca and, in my opinion, it bene-fitted me more than I realised at the time; it let my mind shift to something else. I wanted to get out of bed in the morning because I wanted to know more. For me, it opened up another layer of the world, giving me a different perspective on what I had been going through and making me feel like I had all the power that I needed. If I had the intent and power to perform magick and discover a new path in life, what else was there to discover? Surely, I could conquer depression and deal with my past? Which, thankfully, I did. I came out of the other side much stronger because of it too. Wicca for me did all of the above, as well as teaching me to find my true self – and help others with this too. Yes, other things helped, therapy included, but Wicca built something inside me that I had previously missed out on during my times dealing with mental health issues. We all struggle with aspects of life at times but, truly, Wicca helps me through every day.

10.

Meditation

Meditation is a practice where one typically sits or lies down and focuses on mind, body and soul. Meditation is about achieving a state of awareness in a higher form. It can help you reach a state where you are completely aware of yourself and the moment around you, but your mind is not thinking anything, where you are an observer of your thoughts but you do not let them overwhelm you. Meditation can help you enter your subconscious mind and that can lead you to gain a different perspective on aspects of your life. You can meditate in order to find answers and help you change your frame of mind. Sometimes, thoughts and answers come after meditation so it's always helpful to write down your findings soon after you've finished. Meditation has many benefits; it can help with physical and mental health, reduce stress, anxiety, ageing and many other aspects of your well-being. I would suggest trying meditation to anyone, whatever their faith, as it can be a great benefit to life, as well as a major tool in our Wicca journeys.

MEDITATION AND MAGICK

Meditation can be a really effective tool in Wicca, the Sabbats and Esbats, for magickal workings or even to connect with the universe and the divine.

First, it can help your spell and ritual work – visualising and meditation are key to putting us in the right headspace for magickal practices. (See Part 3, Spell Work, for visualising.) It can help calm you and help you let go of problems and focus completely on the intent for your ritual or spell work.

You may use meditation for looking for answers to elements of your journey, for example you may do a tarot reading, or some form of divination, and the answer you receive from it doesn't make a lot of sense – you can't quite join the dots together about why you have been dealt these cards and how they relate to the situation at hand. So, you may want to take the cards that you received, lay them out in front of you or hold them and meditate on the meanings behind them and how they connect to your life. This will assist in finding the answers.

Meditation can be used with other tools to connect with them – meditate with your wand or athame (ritual tool) to gain a bond with them. Or there could just be an issue you'd like to gain insight into in your life, that you need answers to before using a spell to solve it. You could take a crystal that is relevant for the situation, hold it in one hand and the crystal and its vibrational energy will help you focus more on the subject you have been given and help you find the answer to your problem.

There are many ways you can use meditation in Wicca and you will discover the endless possibilities as your journey continues. With everything in Wicca, practice makes perfect and it may take you a while to be able to reach that perfect state in meditation. So don't be discouraged if it's hard at first, it just takes a little brain training and finding the method that's correct for you to get you there. When you start, I would recommend meditating for around twenty minutes to begin with, it can be very intense. If you're meditating before a spell or ritual and you need to focus on an intent, this could be longer, but make sure your energy is high afterwards for your magick, maybe have a snack and a drink at the ready before you continue.

There are many different ways you can meditate, but let's start with the basics.

MEDITATION METHODS

BASIC MEDITATION

This first method is a great way to begin with meditation techniques.

First, find yourself a place where you will not be disturbed – if it's inside, set the scene, create an area that is relaxing, tidy, a place where nobody can disturb you. (See Part 3, Spell Work for setting the scene.) If it is sunny, you may want to take your meditation outside, this is where I always feel happiest meditating and a lot of Wiccans like to be surrounded by the natural world as it's where they relax and find a balance.

If you are outside, find a quiet place away from the hustle and bustle. Sit on the ground, legs crossed, back straight and let your limbs go limp and heavy. Or alternatively you can lie down, legs straight, arms comfortably placed, or you can sit on a chair.

Close your eyes, take a few deep breaths and, as you do so, with each breath breathe in; as you release your breath, picture all of your thoughts and problems of the day disappearing. Focus on your breath and let your everyday mind and thoughts release themselves and your subconscious take over, until you reach a clear-minded state of higher awareness. If this doesn't come naturally to you, it may take a while, but keep going. If your thoughts seem to take over, focus on your breathing.

Let your subconscious mind take over so that you no longer feel present in the world. Everything is fine and at hand and there's nothing else you need to think about other than your subconscious mind in this time and place. Be and observe the thoughts and feelings you are having, but don't focus on them – you are keeping a clear head.

If there's a situation at hand or a purpose to your meditation, put it in your subconscious mind now. Follow the thoughts you are having and the emotions you are feeling. Sit quietly and focus on it until you acquire the concentration or receive the answers you need.

You may want to set a timer or just let yourself meditate until you feel ready to stop. You can meditate for five minutes or up to an hour, or however long you please.

MOON MEDITATION

Moon meditation, of course, always works best at a full moon, or a specific time of the moon cycle relevant to your intent. Find a comfortable place outside, preferably where you can see the moon. Make sure you are wrapped up warm for this as meditation can sometimes make your body temperature drop.

Follow the basic meditation method: this time once you are into your subconscious mind state, picture the moon up above you and visualise floating up into it and you and the moon becoming one. Explore the energy the moon is surrounding you with.

This method is commonly used to bond with the moon, the goddess and the universe. It can also be used to focus, especially before performing magick, as we do everything by the moon and the sun. We draw down the moon's energy in order to gain concentration and intent for our practices. There are best times of the month in which to meditate, depending on the intent. (See more on the moon in Part 1, Magick and Part 3, Wiccan Holidays and the Wheel of the Year.) Be sure to always drift from the moon and return to yourself and your headspace after you have fulfilled the purpose of your meditation.

OBJECT MEDITATION

Start by following the same method as the basic meditation. If you have the object – it could be a tool you want to bond with or a crystal you are using to help you find answers, your tarot cards or something more personal that you feel will benefit your thoughts and feelings during meditation in order to find the answers you seek. Maybe you're trying to find peace in your mind about a recent break-up, possibly holding some memento of your relationship and meditating with it to find some insight into letting this person go. On the other hand, you could be trying to find an object and wanting to tap into your subconscious in order to find it, and see where you last had it; you may have to just visualise the object in your mind.

The best way to meditate with the object is to get into the state we previously spoke about, where your subconscious mind is taking over your conscious mind, and visualise the object or hold the object in front of you and imagine you are inside it or disappearing into it, as if you and it were becoming one. Receive the energy of the object and what it brings to you, seek what you are looking for and look around inside the object until you find your answer.

MANTRA MEDITATION

This is a meditation during which you say a specific word or sound over and over again and the vibration of the word coordinates your body and the universe. You may have a stereotypical image of meditation, with people sitting cross-legged, meditating while saying the word 'om': this is mantra meditation! You can, of course, say the word 'om', but many people find their own mantra to work with. The best place to do this is outside.

I would recommend drawing down the moon for this and using the moon meditation technique to start with. Reach the part of the moon meditation when you're drawing down the moon and you're about to dissolve into it, then hear a whisper coming from the stars around it – a sound or a single word. This can be used as your mantra. Once you have your mantra, you can meditate with it. Start with the basic meditation method, but instead repeat your mantra slowly over and over again, and then repeat the intent of why you are meditating, then take a deep breath and do it again. Some like to do this just to start off with until their subconscious mind has taken over and their thoughts are where they need to be; some like to do it throughout their meditation because it keeps them regulated with the universe.

BREATHING MEDITATION

This is a very common form of meditation that can be most effective for beginners. Start by repeating the first basic meditation technique up until you have just relaxed your muscles. Now focus on your breathing, focus on how it feels, the timing of it, the sound of it. I always like to focus on my breathing to start with then let it flow naturally. I breathe in for four counts, pushing my stomach out as I do so, then out for four counts, pulling my stomach in as I do this. You can do this for as long as it takes to let your subconscious mind take over. Then focus on the intent of this meditation.

11.

Self-Care

Learning to take time for yourself is extremely important, even if it's just ten minutes each day to take a little 'me' time. So many of us live crazy lives, full of work, fun, hobbies, exercise and travel. Sometimes it's difficult to take just a few minutes to stop and appreciate things and to look after your well-being.

Wicca helps you to take some personal time for yourself. A lot of elements of the faith require making time to stop and focus on your practices and workings in order for them to be effective and making time to explore all of the elements of the wonderful natural world.

There are lot of ways in Wicca we can make time for ourselves that can benefit us; in general, it takes us away from the craziness of life we endure every day, and puts us in our own space to work on our journeys within Wicca, inevitably to make our lives the way we want them to be.

As we discussed in the last chapter, meditation can be an effective way to help you take time for yourself. Meditation places you in a different mindset and gives you time to centre yourself with the universe as well as helping you with Wicca too. I use meditation as a tool within several aspects of my practices – to relax myself and clear my mind, to help me focus, to work through problems and gain insight, and to connect with the divine and elements of the universe.

Also, in Wicca, we obviously have our spell work, rituals and our Sabbats to make time for. When other faiths take a break for their holidays, such as Christmas and Easter, we take the time for our eight Sabbats and our twelve main Esbats. We also take time to celebrate the seasons, the moon, the sun and other natural occurrences. These festivities are fantastic opportunities to celebrate and perform rituals, but also to relax, slow down the pace of life and let yourself re-energise.

Spell and ritual work can require longer periods of time, depending on the complexity of the workings. Plan ahead and set aside a good chunk of time.

Divination can also be a good way of getting away from the outside world and stepping into a calm, focused energy. Most forms of divination require complete concentration and taking time to focus on something specific, taking time to sort through issues and situations you may want to gain insight into. This can be a great way to cope; putting your life in bird's-eye view for a short period of time gives you a second to look over everything in your day, week or month. Divination can be performed at any time, whenever you feel you need to take a second for this. It promotes calm and clarity, strengthening your mind and your focus, and renews energies.

I also feel that Wicca encourages you to explore the outside world, whether it is learning about and searching for a new herb to collect for your next potion, getting outside to do some meditation or looking for a tree to create a wand from. When I go for a walk for any purpose that is to do with Wicca, or even when I just need a break from life and a breath of fresh air, I find that leaving technology behind can help me connect with nature on another level. Many of my practices in Wicca benefit from being away from technology. Even though social media can benefit us in so many ways, it can be a distraction, and freeing your mind from the constant stimulus also helps to calm you.

HOW TO MAKE TIME FOR YOURSELF?

In practice, when it actually comes down to making personal time for yourself, it's not that easy to do. First, managing and organising your life is extremely important; possibly keeping a journal and writing down tasks that you would like to get done today, including your very important downtime, maybe also a Wicca goal for the day. I personally set myself an aim to learn something new within Wicca every weekday. I wake up with the goal in mind and I often do this before bed. I don't have goals at the weekend because less organisation is more relaxing, allowing me to just take things as they come.

Arranging your life a little more and getting your tasks done at a manageable pace can create time. Accept that you are only one person; you can only focus on one thing at a time and you can't grow a flower in a day!

Step back in your day whenever you are able to have a break or a second to breathe and do something nice for yourself, whether it's just getting outside to see the sun, reading a few pages of your favourite book or getting something tasty to eat from a nearby bakery; take a walk and embrace your surroundings.

Also, giving up aspects of your life that no longer serve you can be extremely liberating, creating more time and more mental space. This could mean not checking your phone for an hour in the morning or not wasting your time on something unnecessary that you don't enjoy.

Take self-care seriously. Don't brush it aside and think that it's not important. Whether it is taking time for some divination or meditation, clearing space to make time for your spell or ritual work or even a lovely hot bath every day, see it as important as your other tasks. It can benefit your mental health, Wicca practices and your well-being.

12.

Creativity

Wicca is a faith that encourages creativity and self-expression. Some people like to express their Wicca faith in how they dress; for instance, wearing a pentagram around your neck if you're a Wiccan, pagan or witch. Some also choose to dress with a 'witchy' vibe – lots of black clothing and a black hat to match. You might also incorporate elements of your path into your outfits; for example, people who practise Draconic Wicca may want to incorporate symbols and representations of dragons in their clothing and jewellery, while Green Wiccans might like to wear eco-friendly, natural garments. Some Wiccans like to dress to relate to the Sabbats, maybe wearing colours and symbols that coordinate with the specific celebrations and seasons. Obviously, some Wiccans don't incorporate their faith into their style at all: it's completely up to you.

What I would recommend is to dress to express how you feel on the inside. Wicca can bring out aspects of yourself that you may not have discovered before and, as your confidence grows, it's great to dress in clothing that just makes you happy! Personally, I like to dress according to how I am feeling or to reflect the natural world and relevant celebrations. I might wear lots of black clothing in the winter to represent the cold earth and darker days, and in summer I love bright-yellow dresses covered in sunflowers.

You might be surprised to learn that spell work is another extremely creative element of Wicca. Performing magick is inventive in itself and has elements of self-expression too; everyone finds their own methods of how they like to cast spells and perform rituals. You can also cast spells to simply increase creativity in different elements of your life where you feel it is needed. Also, there is honestly nothing more satisfying (to me, anyway) than creating my own personal magick, potion, spell or ritual. Researching the necessary elements of a spell – herbs, crystals and other ingredients – and then forming it in your own way is in art form in itself. This can bring an overwhelming sense of fulfilment and can make you feel more confident with your magickal practices.

You can also get creative with Wicca in your home, making lots of different hangings, symbols and ornaments with magickal properties or that you can bless, to place around your own personal spaces. You can also display pentagram ornaments and other protective symbols, representations of relevant deities and Wiccan emblems such as the sun, the moon and other elements of nature. Living in an environment which reflects your beliefs can inspire you to express yourself and your faith freely.

The Sabbats also involve many activities that require creating home-made items for your altar and for decoration. Enjoyable activities include painting eggs for Ostara, creating talismans, seasonal wreaths or even dressing up at Samhain, one of the main Sabbats, as your favourite ghoul. The Sabbats also bring great opportunities to get creative with seasonal gifts, such as baked goods and crystals incorporated into jewellery.

You can also be inventive and resourceful when it comes to creating your tools. Even though, nowadays, tools are easily available to purchase, many Wiccans still prefer to make their own because they believe that it adds to the bond between them and their special items. An example of this might be a wand. Lots of Wiccans and witches like to make their wands from scratch, initially collecting the wood at the tree, through to decorating them with symbols, feathers, paint and crystals. You can create pretty much any tool that you might want to use from the natural world; you can search for beautiful shells to burn your incense in or collect stones to mark or decorate to make into runes. The possibilities found in the wild are endless. Wicca is about using what is around you, not about how much money you have to spend.

As I mentioned in pages 56–7, getting creative with your Book of Shadows can also be lots of fun! I like to decorate each page to correspond with the particular subject, filling it with drawings, paintings, colourful items and dried flowers. I'm an extremely visual person, and I'm aware that everything that I see can affect my mood. So, creating my Book of Shadows to reflect my experiences and ideas, using relevant, imaginative visuals, gives me great satisfaction. Opportunities for creativity are endless within Wicca; it excites and inspires you, helping you to express parts of yourself in ways that you possibly cannot even imagine.

13.

Kindness

The law of three really made me realise how important kindness is, to yourself and to others. Remember the fundamental Wiccan teaching, 'If it harms none, do what you will'. Whenever I have debated doing something when I wasn't sure if I was acting with good intentions, I always looked to the law of three to help me determine if my actions were correct. It taught me that being kind doesn't just benefit others, but how I feel about myself and the earth too. It also affects how others felt about me and their support for me; this has helped me enormously in life. The law taught me not to act out of anger or sadness, because that energy would return to me. This doesn't mean that you *can't* be angry or sad; these are natural feelings that everyone has, but there are other ways to deal with strong negative emotions and other solutions that don't cause more harm. Sometimes it is overwhelmingly difficult to follow this, but fighting bad with bad doesn't make it good, nor does it solve anything.

A large part of Wicca is understanding that there *is* balance in this earth, bad and good, and accepting it, realising that there can be no good without bad and the only way to move past it is to treat bad with good. If aspects of your life lose that balance, it can end in your unhappiness. This doesn't mean you have to let people be horrible to you and be kind to them in return; simply walking away or trying to understand other people's anger can help both parties and benefit your well-being and theirs. Life can throw you confusing and frustrating situations. When I am confused or angry about someone's actions, meditation on the subject helps me find peace with it and understanding for the other parties, and this helps me to solve the situation in my mind. It's always good to give yourself time to think over a situation that may upset you, think about solutions and allow yourself to calm down before acting, go with your instinct and solve it in the most balanced way that you can.

Wicca also encourages a sense of positivity that many people struggle to find. It gives you a sense of freedom which, throughout childhood and most of your teenage life, is sometimes hard to feel. It gives you freedom to take a path you want within the faith and gives you time to have all to yourself.

THE IMPORTANCE OF KINDNESS

Being kind and spreading positive energy may sound like a hippy-dippy cliché, but it can truly benefit yourself and others in many ways and create a certain mentality that allows you to conquer challenging situations relatively easily. Remembering kindness and compassion to yourself and to other people can create balance that can benefit mental health and strengthen your Wicca practice.

Obviously the law of three applies here; if you put out positivity and are kind and balanced, that energy can return to you three times, in all situations. For example, if you cheat on someone, this will hurt that person – even if they have done wrong too, the chances are you're not treating them correctly. This action or the energies around this action will return to you, causing you *more* harm or further problems surrounding the situation, whereas if you no longer love them and want to be with someone else, leave them in a kind way, explaining yourself fairly, honestly and how you deem appropriate and that energy you put out there will return back to you.

It can also help with energy within Wicca. Having a positive energy and putting out positive energy can help with the accuracy of your spells; we all have down days, but being kind can help keep silly minor problems at bay, which allows you to focus on your craft and your faith. Getting rid of these negative aspects in your life and focusing on the kinder, more honest approach will solve a lot and prevent future problems with the situations you have at hand, and allow you to focus on what is real. It's important to remember nobody is below or above you, and if you encounter people that treat you as if you are not worth their time, remember they will get their energy returned to them; this allows you to focus on the divine and helps you to be more considerate to other humans, animals and the earth.

Also, putting out negative energy all the time can allow other negative energies/shadows and spirits to feed off it, draining your power and other positive energy you may hold. I was an extremely confused younger teen who made a lot of mistakes, and it took me a while to note that I was just running a vicious circle around myself, making my life and well-being increasingly worse. I was never a 'bad' person – I never wanted to hurt anyone and I've always felt extremely guilty about the smallest of things, but I was extremely confused. There were many times when someone would be unkind to me or I was thrown a situation that hurt me and it would confuse me. I'd think, how can they say that to me? Why are they doing this? Why is this happening? And I would act out of anger, fighting them with negativity because I had no idea how to deal with the situation otherwise – and that continued in a cycle because I was completely unaware that the world was actually not against me; I just had life thrown at me, didn't know how to handle it and made it a lot worse instead of dealing with it correctly – problems all teenagers and young adults face.

Even before I discovered Wicca, I realised the fault in my actions. I was having an argument with an old friend about something irrelevant, which at the time seemed so important, and we were both angry. I knew I had done wrong and so had she. So I stopped, apologised for my anger and asked her why she was upset. I apologised for my actions and also explained my upset. She soon realised the way she'd hurt me and we worked out our issues.

If I'm angry and I decide to tweet about someone or bitch about someone behind their back, it's going to cause issues and the people involved will react badly. So, I simply stopped and it changed everything; there were some issues I removed from my life, like people who just wanted to cause negativity and situations I was unhappy with, but as time went by things improved, problems didn't seem to be as frequent, I felt happier and started to enjoy my life instead of worrying about petty arguments and negativity.

Being kind changed my perspective on everything and created a calm life for me which relieved issues I didn't even think being 'kind' could affect. Then, upon discovering the law of three, it made sense finally – the way I felt and my actions – and helped me improve even more. All I sought was tolerance and love. I wanted acceptance, happiness, love for myself and people to love and, upon seeking this, I got it. There are actions you can take to be more kind – studying the law of three is a great place to start.

WAYS TO BE MORE KIND

☾ Try to understand. When you're in a situation where you are adamant that you are correct it can be confusing and hard to see the other person's point of view, especially if you are not on good terms with this person. Really try to put yourself in someone else's shoes and see the issues that they're facing – this can help you sort the problems and, if you have to, let go of the issues and walk away.

☾ Don't fight bad with bad. The old saying 'kill with kindness' can truly be the cure; even if it pains you to do so, it can remove the problems completely and prevent problems for the future. For example, if somebody says something unkind about your appearance, understand where it is coming from. It's not about you at all; unkind remarks are *always* about the person who is making them. It's possibly jealously and anger built up inside of them. Instead of making a rude remark back to them about their appearance, simply say something like, 'I really like how I look, I feel super great today; you look nice too', even if you have to *grit* your teeth while doing so and this person irks you to your very core. This removes their power – and they may realise that they were being unkind or just think twice about being unkind to you again. I'm not saying don't stand up for yourself, rather just speak the absolute truth and express your opinions with positivity.

☾ Be more kind to all living things, not just humans. Understanding the earth and realising that you need to take care of it and give thanks to it is a valuable consideration for all people which also reaps benefits, as the earth then repays you. Similarly, treating animals in a kind, loving and respectful way benefits you because they give love back and because of how that makes you feel. Everything is made from the same matter – humans, animals and the natural world.

☾ This can also create understanding for humans too, helping you understand diversity within people, which is very important – you can't have respect for just one person, then hate everything else, because we are all made up from the same elements. To hate one thing would be to hate everything. Remember, without any aspect of this earth, there would not be another. We are all just as important as each other, no matter our race, our gender, our sexuality, and we should be proud of each other and love each other in the way we would like in return.

☾ Stop dealing with your problems in an unhealthy way. Yes, this means stop tweeting about people, stop making indirect comments about people online, stop speaking unkindly about people behind their backs and stop creating problems that don't exist. Many aspects of Wicca can help you with this and also help you to find the true meaning of your problems and stop creating fake ones. If you have a problem, and you're confused about what to do, explore avenues regarding how to sort it, don't make it worse because you're angry. That will only cause more hurt and further problems. If you have an issue, deal with it face on, speak to people in a kind manner and try to resolve matters. Don't let it fester inside you and ruin your mental health, thereby causing more problems.

Part
3

How to Get Started

It is incredibly easy to begin your Wicca journey as soon as you feel ready. Wicca is not about having the correct equipment or mastering extremely difficult techniques, and you might be surprised at how easily it becomes a part of your life.

14.

Wiccan Holidays and the Wheel of the Year

In Wicca, we follow the natural occurrences of the universe and we do everything by the earth's natural cycle. The Wheel or the Wheel of the Year is a circle of time; it's a cycle of seasons, of birth, growth and death. It represents the full cycle of the seasons according to the sun.

As you know, the same natural occurrences happen every year. We have a cold winter, where the days become shorter and the nights get longer and the sun dims for a period of time. Then the sun is born again, and the wheel turns and spring comes around. There is life sprouting from our earth and the world gets to its peak of fertility. Then summer comes along and growth, life and warmth are at their peak. Then autumn arrives and the warm earth begins to cool, we feel the cold returning and the earth goes into hibernation, and then the next year this amazing cycle happens all over again. The Wheel of the Year is made up of eight sections or eight main natural changes in the earth that we all celebrate; these are called the Sabbats. By marking and celebrating these festivals it also helps us synchronise with the earth.

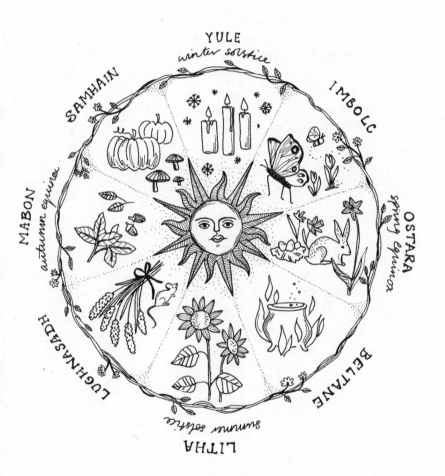

THE SABBATS

The Sabbats are in essence 'Wiccan holidays' that almost all Wiccans and some witches celebrate. Instead of following the holidays that are related to Christian festivals, we celebrate the traditionally pagan festivals that many of the Christian festivals were adapted from. There are eight Sabbat celebrations which all tie in to the four seasons of the year, winter, spring, summer and autumn. The Sabbats are here to help us celebrate the natural world and the earth's cycle that we couldn't live without, while also honouring our faith and practices and our deities. We celebrate all aspects of life and death and everything that they bring. There are four main Sabbats: Samhain, Imbolc, Beltane and Lammas (Lughnasadh). These greater Sabbats always occur when the earth's energy is at its peak. They were traditionally known as the 'fire festivals' honouring the sun gods. The lesser Sabbats mark the points where one season transitions to the next, the astronomical beginning of a new season. They always occur on the solstice or equinox. Solstice is a term for the two occasions of the year when the sun is directly above either the furthest point north or the furthest point south of the equator that it ever reaches. The equinox is a term for another twice-yearly occurrence when the sun crosses the equator, so day and night are at equal lengths.

YULE (LESSER SABBAT)

Also known as the winter solstice

WHEN IS YULE?

On the shortest day and longest night of the year

Northern hemisphere
20–24 December

Southern hemisphere
20–23 June

WHAT IS YULE?

Yule, also known as the winter solstice, is the celebration of the shortest day and longest night of the year. The sun reaches its southernmost point in the sky in the Wheel of the Year's cycle. Yule is the celebration of the abundance of light, we are celebrating even though the darkness has taken over our green earth; we are aware that from this day forward the days will become lighter. Also, the sun king is now returning and will begin to thrive. It's a time for renewal in all aspects and makes us aware that the brighter, longer days are near. At this time, fires were traditionally burnt by the Celts in order to frighten off the wintery cold and to welcome the sun.

HOW TO CELEBRATE IT

If you are not aware, Christmas as we know it was traditionally the pagan holiday Yule. Many ways that you can celebrate Yule are similar to the ways that Christmas is traditionally celebrated. So, you can decorate pine trees and yule logs etc. as many of these rituals are meaningful to both holidays. There are *tons* of things you can do and everyone will have their own way of celebrating just as many people have their own individual ways of celebrating Thanksgiving or Christmas. Here are a few ideas:

ACTIVITIES

☾ Decorate a Yule tree: around this time of year it's a tradition for pagans to bring pine trees into their homes and hang food on them for wandering spirits, so that on the coldest day of the year the spirits have somewhere to reside and food for this day and night.

☾ Start planning for the future and the warmer days to come.

☾ Write your goals for the next year in your Book of Shadows.

☾ Plan spells that you would like to try out in the coming months.

☾ Make plans for your herb garden.

☾ Burn small pieces of pine in a cauldron for good luck in the new year.

☾ Bring old pine into your home, for protection and protection spells.

☾ Create an evergreen wreath to hang on your door. This represents continuous life on this earth, how life and warmth will always return to the Wheel of the Year even after a long and cold winter. The wreath can be created with mistletoe (fabulous for healing, protection and this plant represents growth and fertility). Or you can simply have mistletoe in your home too to symbolise these positive properties. Holly can be combined with mistletoe, as it represents the marriage of the sun returning to earth. Holly is also amazing for its protective purposes alone. Ivy, which can represent everlasting life, including growth of the natural earth, can also be included. Of course, you could also include many other seasonal plants and maybe create the base from pine; this is amazing for protection, particularly relevant to this Sabbat.

☾ Celebrate the Sabbat with a meal with Yule-related food for your loved ones.

☾ Sing solstice carols.

☾ Spells such as fire spells, prosperity spells, new beginnings, Yuletide charms, and peace and luck for the months to come, are all great to cast at this time.

ALTAR IDEAS

Decorate your altar at this time of the year with relevant decorations to honour the Sabbat and give thanks to you deities.

• Make use of the seasonal colours of red, white, black and green. They represent warmth and the darkest and coldest night of the year, as well as the warmer green days that are on their way.

- Mistletoe
- Pine cones
- Ivy
- Yule log
- White and black ribbons represent the cold and dark days surrounding you.
- Though it might seem irrelevant, pictures of the sun can be great; this welcomes the sun king back and honours the warmer days to come.

FOOD AND DRINK

Good foods and drinks for around this time of year are anything with strong, warm and spicy flavours. This honours and welcomes the return of the sun, while also warming you up. Suggestions are:

- Spicy food such as curries
- Cinnamon-flavoured or spiced cakes
- Ginger tea
- Hot apple cider
- Spiced mulled wine or wassail
- Seasoned soups
- Spiced buttermilk bread
- Nuts

CRYSTALS

Relevant crystals to carry around with you this time of the year, to meditate with, to use in divination and spell work and to place at your altar are:

- Bloodstone
- Clear quartz
- Emerald
- Garnet
- Citrine

HERBS

Herbs that are relevant at this time of the year are seasonal plants and also those that represent warmth. You can dry these herbs at your altar for future use; they're amazing for cooking and making teas (depending on what they are and if they're edible) as well as using them for magickal workings too.

- Mistletoe
- Fir
- Oak leaves
- Pine needles
- Camomile
- Cinnamon
- Cloves
- Nutmeg

INCENSE

You might need incense to use around Yule time during casting circles, burning at your altar, for cleansing and consecrating, as well as for magickal workings. Good examples are:

- Cinnamon
- Cedar wood
- Pine (all winter tree scents)
- Bayberry
- Frankincense

IMBOLC (GREATER SABBAT)

Also known as Brigid's Day or Candlemas

WHEN IS IMBOLC?

Northern hemisphere
2 February
Southern hemisphere
2 August

WHAT IS IMBOLC?

Imbolc, or Brigid's Day, is a celebration of the earth waking up and warming up; it is a preparation for spring. Winter is coming to an end and the sun king is becoming stronger. We are celebrating that the days are beginning to become brighter and we are preparing and planning what needs to be done for when new life comes. It's a good time to pick yourself up from the winter blues and shake any negativity off. It's time for us to honour the Triple Goddess, while she is in her maiden form and is warming up the cold earth with the seed of spring gathering in her womb. It's a beneficial time for Wiccans to start sparks of activity in different aspects of their lives which they may have found it difficult to focus on in the gloomy winter months. Anything that you would like to begin to concentrate on or direct energy to in your practices or personal life should start to be included in the mix now. It's also a great time to let go of any unnecessary aspects of your life you may have been carrying on your shoulders for a while. It's a time to clear away any old and unwanted thoughts, feelings and situations and to make room for the new. Anything that you need to eliminate to help you see a future path that you are embarking on more clearly as the world warms up. It's also a day to honour the goddess, Brigid; she is the goddess of fire, the sun and the hearth. She will begin to bring fertility and growth as the sun king begins to warm the cold earth up.

HOW TO CELEBRATE IT

As you might imagine, Imbolc celebrations centre around new life and cleansing.

ACTIVITIES

☾ Begin to spring clean. Clear your room, house and workplace and get rid of things that no longer serve you and are of no use. This will start to prepare you for the hustle and bustle of the spring and summer months.

☾ Also, clear any emotional baggage you may be carrying – situations, relationships, people, stressful memories. This will help you make room for the positive new beginnings that are coming your way soon.

☾ If you wish, this is a good time to clear and sort out your altar. If there are any tools or anything at your altar that you are not happy with, or you simply would just like to have a change around, now is the time to do it. Collect new tools, begin to connect with them if this is what you wish to do, now is the perfect time.

☾ Begin to plant seeds in your magickal herb garden in preparation for spring. If you are don't already have a herb garden, this is the perfect time to begin planting and creating a garden.

☾ You could also go out and plant seeds in wild places, near trees, etc.

☾ Create a Brigid's cross: this is a symbol of fire which can be used for protection. It is made from leftover dead reeds that might be lying around in your garden or by rivers and fields. You can hang the cross at your door or place it at your altar. After you are finished with your Brigid's cross, you can bury it or set fire to it for good luck and to welcome the sun as it begins to wake up again.

☾ A Brigid's doll is created to bring luck to your home around this time. You create these dolls from grass, reeds and sticks. There are lots of different ways you can use this doll for protection; some like to make it and then welcome it into their home and have it there for the duration of Imbolc, welcoming in the goddess Brigid's energy. Then, after Imbolc has come to an end, they bury the doll or lay it to rest near a tree.

☾ If you are a new witch, Imbolc is a great time for self-dedication ceremonies and initiations.

ℭ Some like to leave food out for Brigid (see below for some ideas) at their altar to welcome her energies into your home.

ℭ Go for a walk and search for signs of spring, collect new stones to use for your circles, etc.

ℭ Create a bonfire or light a fire such as a yellow, gold or white candle to welcome the sun god as he awakens.

ALTAR IDEAS

- Snowdrops – these beautiful pure flowers are the first sign of spring, which is a huge sign of Imbolc.
- Your Brigid's crosses and dolls can remain at your altar until Imbolc comes to a close.
- Swan feathers or fake white feathers represent life, faithfulness and loyalty.
- Sheep decorations like yarn sheep toys or wool or fake wool are good to keep at your altar at this time.
- Oil lamps and candles in the colours of white, gold, yellow and green are appropriate; they hold Brigid's warm energies within, to welcome the sun god and to represent the cold earth warming up and green earth that is to come.
- Orange, red and yellow ribbons honour the sun god and the warm earth to come.

FOOD AND DRINK

Good foods and drinks to eat around this time of the year are anything that represents growth, because that's one of the main reasons that we celebrate this Sabbat. Also, seasonal foods such as spring vegetables and fruit are relevant.

- Seeds, such as sunflower and pumpkin, and seed-related foods
- Poppy seed cakes and bread and any other seeded bread
- Oats

- Dairy or dairy replacements, such as sheep's and goat's milk and cheese (since the traditional Imbolc Sabbat was the start of the lambing season)
- Garlic, peppers, onions and olives
- Also baked goods such as scones, breads, muffins, waffles and pancakes

CRYSTALS

Relevant crystals to carry around with you this time of the year and to meditate with, to use in divination and spell work and to place at your altar are:

- Amethyst
- Yellow tourmaline
- Citrine
- Bloodstone
- Ruby
- Garnet
- Turquoise

HERBS

Herbs and plants that are good for this time of the year are fresh spring herbs, ones that start to blossom at the beginning of this season. You can dry these herbs at your altar for future use, they're amazing to use for cooking and making teas (depending on what they are and if they're edible) as well as using for magickal workings too.

- Blackberry
- Snowdrops
- Witch hazel
- Lemongrass
- Camomile
- Cinnamon
- Coriander

Good incense to use during casting circles, burning at your altar around Imbolc time and for cleansing and consecrating, as well as magickal workings, are:

- Vanilla
- Carnation
- Basil
- Bay
- Myrrh
- Spring flower scents

OSTARA (LESSER SABBAT)

Also known as spring equinox

WHEN IS OSTARA?

Northern hemisphere
19–22 March

Southern hemisphere
19–22 September

WHAT IS OSTARA?

Ostara is a celebration of the start of spring, it's when night and day have become at perfect balance with each other. At this time, light now begins to take over darkness. Signs of spring are here for most of us or are arriving very soon. New life and growth are appearing all around us. Winter is drawing to an end and it's getting to the time where we need to shake off the winter, if we haven't already at Imbolc, and move full force ahead. All of the planning and procrastinating at Imbolc is now to be put to the test and begun. It's a time for fertility, new growth, the birth of animals and insects too. The sun is slowly awakening to its full potential. The sun god and the young maiden goddess are married now and so conception is imminent. When she gives birth she will become the great mother. It's also time to begin to honour your spring deities and your fertility deities, the main one being the Germanic Anglo-Saxon goddess Ostara who the Sabbat is named after. She wakes up the earth with her powerful energy and creates fertility, growth and renewal all around. Ostara often takes the form of a hare or rabbit, which is why rabbits are a huge symbol of Ostara.

HOW TO CELEBRATE IT

Easter, the traditional Christian holiday that is widely celebrated, has been adapted from the pagan Sabbat Ostara. As you may know, Easter is named after the female hormone oestrogen, necessary for fertility, which is one of the main aspects of the celebration of Ostara. As Easter has evolved from Ostara, there are actually quite a few similarities between the two holidays.

ACTIVITIES

☾ Any plans or goals that you would like to complete this year, get started on them now; motivation is high!

☾ Start your magickal herb garden if you haven't already, if you don't have room, no worries! Small pots and plants in appropriate places can be just as effective.

☾ Take a walk, look for the first inspirational and motivational signs of spring. Maybe even press a flower or two.

☾ Hold an Ostara egg hunt.

☾ Wear green to represent the green earth arriving.

☾ Spells to cast at this time would be for hope, love and good fortune or any that relate to achieving goals, to fertility and to love.

☾ Bless an egg with a property of your choice and eat it.

ALTAR IDEAS

- Decorate it with green, purple and yellow ribbons to represent the spring and greenery that comes to the earth.
- Light green, purple, yellow and orange candles.

- Paint real or fake eggs for your altar to represent fertility and honour the fertility goddess Ostara.
- Decorate your altar with some spring flowers – only pick a few though! After picking flowers, water them to give thanks and plant some more seeds around them if you can.
- Pot up a plant and place it at your altar, keep it healthy and watch it grow and flourish.
- Add statues, trinkets or stuffed toys of hares or rabbits – these are major symbols of fertility and immortality, and are close representations of fertility deities.

FOOD AND DRINK

Good foods and drinks for this time of the year are anything that represent fertility and seasonal foods to honour the beginning of spring:

- Green vegetables
- Seeds
- Eggs
- Dairy such as goat's, cow's and sheep's cheese and milk. Free-range or home-produced is best, but shop-bought or dairy substitutes, if you don't eat dairy, are just as good.
- Meats such as lamb, ham and rabbit, or meat substitutes
- Flowers that are edible, on salads, etc.
- Light breads
- Fresh juices

CRYSTALS

Relevant crystals to carry around with you this time of the year and to meditate with, use in divination and spell work, and place at your altar are:

- Clear quartz
- Agate
- Rose quartz
- Amazonite

- Jasper
- Lapis lazuli

Herbs and flowers that are preferable at this time of the year are seasonal flowers and herbs that can be planted, or that begin to blossom or be fragrant in the spring.

- Lilies
- Narcissus
- Lavender
- Honeysuckle
- Lemon balm
- Daffodils

Good incense to use during casting circles, burning at your altar around Ostara time and for cleansing and consecrating, as well as for magickal workings, are:

- Floral – spring flowers
- Rose
- Strawberry
- Oak moss
- Sandalwood

BELTANE (GREATER SABBAT)

Also known as May Day

Northern hemisphere
31 April – 1 May
It can be celebrated either day or is traditionally celebrated from the night of 31 April until the day of 1 May

Southern hemisphere

31 October – 1 November

Beltane is celebrated because we are now at the peak of spring; the sun god has now taken over. For many of us, summer is arriving, or is coming very soon. It's a super joyous, happy, exciting day that honours life. The earth is buzzing and all of the earth's energies are thriving; fertility, sexuality, passion, energy and new life are at their peak of stimulation at this time. Fertility is the main theme for Beltane. The Triple Goddess in her maiden form and the Horned God are finally united and they are bringing new life onto the earth. It's the time of the year when we need to grant luck to the summer months and the growth that is coming. It is one of the solar festivals, the other being Samhain. Beltane represents birth, while Samhain represents death, which is why Beltane is seen as the most important cele-bration by some people.

HOW TO CELEBRATE IT

Beltane celebrations focus on fertility, abundance and all of the amazing gifts that the earth gives us at this time.

ACTIVITIES

☾ Create amulets made from rose quartz and give them to loved ones, friends and family. This is a gift that can help with positivity and passion and they can help to lower anxiety too. For specific loved ones this can help with the passion and romance between the two of you and it can also calm nerves!

☾ Flowers and greenery are a huge part of Beltane.

☾ Create flower crowns.

☾ Create daisy chains.

☾ Wear flowers on your body.

☾ Make a green man mask from leaves.

☾ Beltane is a time of love, so if you have a loved one that you would like to make a commitment to, this is an excellent time for marriage, handfasting and promise rituals. You may want to plan your ceremony for Beltane.

☾ Dance round a maypole; this is a pole that is typically made from wood or metal and that has ribbons tied to a wreath around it. The maypole is a phallic symbol of the male, the wreath around it and the ribbons coming off it, the vagina. We are celebrating fertility and the marriage of the two of them around this time! You can do a traditional maypole dance around this pole holding the ribbons. Look out for nearby maypole festivities – there are probably more than you think; if not you could create one yourself with your loved ones or your coven.

☾ As this is a day of love, if you are of an appropriate age, comfortable and have a partner you would like to partake in this with, being sexually active is part of the celebration – this is an amazing time to do this.

☾ Also if you have plans to conceive, now is a great and lucky time!

☾ Be safe, be comfortable and never do this if you don't want to!

☾ Another way to celebrate love is just to go for a walk – you could search for a hawthorn tree, make a wish, have a picnic and collect some wild flowers. Share this experience with a friend or loved one or enjoy a solitary walk.

☾ Spells to cast at this time are love spells and vitality, protection, romance and purification spells. Casting your circles with oats around this time of the year is also a good idea! They are a traditional Beltane grain for good luck.

☾ Light a Beltane fire – have a Beltane fire ritual with your friends and family, serve food and have an outside bonfire. Fires are traditionally to honour our sun gods, and celebrate the warmth and the sun god taking over the cold.

ALTAR IDEAS

- Decorate it with seasonal spring flowers.
- Drape it with green cloth and ribbons to represent the green earth as it is now here!
- Add birch and hawthorn branches, burnt in your cauldron.
- Light red, pink and green candles.
- Red and pink represent passion, love and fertility, which suit the theme of Beltane.

FOOD AND DRINK

- Oats in all forms: oat cookies, oatmeal, oat bread
- Dairy, cheeses and milks or dairy-free alternatives
- Also spicy food, to represent the element of fire and the sun
- May Day wine
- Vanilla-flavoured foods
- Fairy cakes
- Ice cream
- Sweet breads
- Elderflower and other flowery-flavoured cordials

CRYSTALS

Relevant crystals to carry around with you this time of the year and to meditate with, use in divination and spell work, place at your altar and, around Beltane, give as gifts to loved ones and partners, are:

- Rose quartz
- Emerald
- Sunstone
- Pink tourmaline
- Beryl
- Pink angel aura quartz

Any herbs and flowers that are blooming now where you live are perfect for Beltane. Try to get the most vibrant and powerful blossoming herbs to work with at this time of the year.

- Lilac
- Thistle
- Flaxseed
- Paprika
- Hawthorn
- Rowan
- Daffodil
- Honeysuckle

INCENSE

Good incense to use during casting circles, burning at your altar around Beltane time and for cleansing and consecrating, as well as for magickal workings, are:

- Peach
- Rose
- Vanilla
- Jasmine

LITHA (LESSER SABBAT)

Midsummer, or summer solstice

WHEN IS LITHA?

Northern hemisphere
20–24 June
It is typically celebrated on the longest day and the shortest night of the year

Southern hemisphere
20–24 December

WHAT IS LITHA?

Litha is the celebration of the longest day and the shortest night of the year. The sun god is thriving and at his most vibrant peak, giving warmth to the earth and growth all around. We are celebrating the potential and successes that surround us. From now on the days will begin to become shorter again and darkness will begin to take over. The summer and warmth are still sticking around for a while, though, and it is still a very happy occasion. We are celebrating the pregnancy of the Triple Goddess with the Horned God. The Oak King is currently ruling the waxing half of the year while the Holly King is ruling the waning half of the year. The Holly King and the Oak King are battling with each other and the Holly King will eventually overrule the Oak King. Litha is a time for important magick and major spell work that needs to be put into action; it's the best time to complete any huge magickal workings that need tackling. Before the darker days return, we must celebrate.

HOW TO CELEBRATE IT

Litha comes at such a positive time of year and your celebrations will reflect this.

ACTIVITIES

☾ Tackle the most challenging and most anticipated spells and rituals at midsummer, the ones that require the most energy from you; what better time to do it than when the world's energies are at their peak! It's the best time of the year for rituals to do with fire, faery magick, love, passion, energy and luck for the warmer times to come.

☾ It's also a good time to renew any tools or create or purchase any extra magickal tools you may require.

☾ Throw a midsummer bonfire or have a fire ritual. Or organise an outside gathering to simply enjoy the sun! There are loads of different ways that you can do this, a traditional midsummer bonfire would (obviously) be outside, although if this is not an option, a wood burner inside would also be fine. Burn pieces of old oak, light them on the evening before midsummer, then let them burn out as they reach the morning. It is also common to scatter herbs on the fire. Some Wiccans also burn the nine sacred types of wood (birch, rowan, ash, alder, willow, hawthorn, oak, holly and hazel) to bring them good luck and a good harvest. During the midsummer bonfire they would jump over the fire, then let the fire burn down *completely* and sometimes collect ashes from the fire and scatter them on the fields or on their herb garden to bring good fortune in the harvesting season coming in the near future. You could also keep some ashes for luck within spell work or rituals.

☾ Create a god's eye: it is typically made from wool or string and its purpose is to give protection and luck for the darker and colder days to come. Hang the god's eye above your altar or on your door.

☾ Go for a walk and enjoy the peak of summer! Collect things from the natural world that you need for magickal workings and to place at your altar. Have a picnic or barbecue or even just go to the beach or go for a bike ride.

☾ If you work with the fae or just like to appreciate them, midsummer is the time for the faery rede. At this time, the fae will be riding magickal animals across the countryside, so hang out, either outside your house or in a nearby field. Bells and offerings such as sparkly decorations and food can be used to create the perfect area for the fae.

- Light green, yellow, gold and red candles to represent the sun god at his peak and the green earth at its fullest.
- Decorate your altar with summer flowers such as sunflowers, carnations, poppies and hydrangeas.
- Place a ring of flowers around your altar or around specific items for protection.
- Pictures of the sun or ornaments symbolising the sun honour the sun god being at his peak.
- Oak leaves represent the Oak King, who has been ruling for this half of the year, but will be laid to rest soon. Oak in different forms can be relevant to Litha.
- Gold, yellow and orange ribbons and cloth can be draped at your altar.

FOOD AND DRINK

- Warm-coloured vegetables such as butternut squash, sweet potato, carrots and tomatoes are all great to eat around this time of the year. They represent warmth and the wonderful produce we receive from the summer.
- Home-grown or locally produced leafy green vegetables
- Spicy foods
- Curries
- Spiced cakes
- Spiced punch and rum
- Anything with honey or as an alternative golden or maple syrup – bees are another representation of Litha, the midsummer full moon is actually also known as the honey moon!
- Barbecued food or flame-grilled food is good to eat too; once again it represents the heat and the sun's energy.
- Ice cream – not only is it cooling in the summer months, it also represents the colder days to come.

CRYSTALS

Relevant crystals to carry around with you this time of the year, to meditate with, to use in divination and spell work, and to place at your altar are:

- Emerald
- Sunstone
- Citrine
- Yellow tourmaline
- Yellow topaz
- Calcite

HERBS

Seasonal fresh herbs are great for Litha, as is anything that represents heat, flavour and greenery and ties in with Litha's celebrations.

- Mint
- Basil
- Rosemary
- Sage
- Honeysuckle
- Carnation
- Paprika

INCENSE

Good incense to use during casting circles and burning at your altar around Litha time and for cleansing and consecrating, as well as for magickal workings, are:

- Lavender
- Citrus scents, such as orange and lemon
- Musk
- Pine
- Rose
- Summer flowers

LAMMAS

Also known as Lughnasadh

Northern hemisphere
1 August

Southern hemisphere
1 February

WHAT IS LAMMAS?

Lammas is a celebration of harvest; it's the realisation that the green earth's energies and bustling growth are beginning to slow down, darker and colder days will arrive soon and summer is coming to an end. The warm days are still lingering, the sun god is losing his strength; he is finishing putting his energies into the earth now, producing the first of the two harvests, but he has not yet come to an end. The goddess's condition has now changed; she is the grain mother. She will dry the crops and let the seeds fall from them into the earth now, where they will rest all through winter, returning at Imbolc. The main theme of Lammas is fulfilment: the earth is producing a harvest and providing us with food.

HOW TO CELEBRATE IT

Lammas celebrations reflect the achievements of the physical, mental, emotional and creative labours of the last few months.

ACTIVITIES

☾ Create a corn mother or a corn dolly. These can be made from things left over from the first harvest in the fields – corn, reeds, wheat, etc.

☾ Relevant spells to cast at this time of the year are for abundance, connection, career, mental or physical gain. Cast your circle with relevant grains such as oats, corn and wheat; this can strengthen your circle.

☾ Also, if you have any spells where you require the sun's energies, cast them now!

☾ This is a time for fulfilment, especially when it comes from the harvest.

☾ Create a meal for your loved ones with all the home-grown food you may have produced in your garden and herb garden.

☾ This is the last opportunity of the year to enjoy the outdoors, while there is still some warmth, so if you haven't already done so, go on picnics, walks, bike rides and visits to the beach. Go out and collect fallen seeds from nearby fields, parks and paths and plant them ready for next Imbolc.

☾ This is a perfect time for you to create your broom, gathering old twigs, reeds and wood which are easy to find at Lammas. They're an amazing magickal tool and a representation of fulfilment and home.

☾ Perform Lammas harvesting rituals to honour the sun god for the last time.

ALTAR IDEAS

- Light gold, yellow, brown, orange and black candles to represent the earth changing from green to brown, autumnal colours, and black for the darker days arriving.
- Tie ribbons and drape cloth at your altar, in the colours gold, yellow, orange and brown. You can also wear these colours to honour the Sabbat.
- Scatter relevant grains from the harvest to honour the fulfilment you feel at this time of the year: wheat, corn, onion, oats, barley and rye.
- Sunflowers are now at their growing peak. Potted marigolds are wonderful to grow at your altar too.
- Place your corn mother or corn dolly at your altar.

FOOD AND DRINK

- Home-made bread made from wheat, corn, rye and oats
- Fresh berries and fresh fruit from the recent harvest
- Fruity berry wines
- Home-grown vegetables and fruits
- Sweetcorn, popcorn, corn on the cob, any corn-related produce
- Apples, apple cider and apple cake

CRYSTALS

Relevant crystals to carry around with you this time of the year, to meditate with, to use in divination and spell work and to place at your altar are:

- Citrine
- Clear quartz
- Aventurine
- Golden topaz
- Cat's eye

HERBS, FLOWERS, GRAINS AND BERRIES

Herbs, flowers and anything that has come from the recent harvest. As with all of the Sabbats, you can dry these herbs at your altar, around this time, for future use. They're amazing to use for cooking and making teas (depending on what they are and if they're edible), as well as using for magickal workings.

- All grains
- Meadowsweet
- Mint
- Heather
- Sloes

Good incense to use during casting circles, burning at your altar around Lammas time and for cleansing and consecrating, as well as magickal workings, are:

- Sandalwood
- Rose
- Camomile
- Mint

MABON

Also known as the autumn equinox

WHEN IS MABON?

Northern hemisphere
21–24 September

Southern hemisphere
21–24 March

WHAT IS MABON?

Mabon is a celebration of balance – the days and the nights are now in equilibrium once again. It's time to give thanks to what the summer has brought us and the warmer days that have just passed. This is the second harvest Sabbat; the harvest is coming to an end soon. It's also time to let go of anything that you may be clinging on to; projects are now coming to an end. We harvest the last of our herb gardens and lay everything to rest. It's similar to a pagan Thanksgiving. The goddess has now begun to lie down to rest for the winter. The harvest lord, or the green man, is sacrificed and he falls into the earth, his seeds lie there until next spring.

Celebrations at this time focus on the awesome way that the natural world gives us stability, harmony and equilibrium.

ACTIVITIES

☾ Create a horn of plenty, also called a cornucopia. This is a symbol of what the harvest has given us. You can buy a shaped cone or wicker basket or create your own if you want to give it a go. Fill the basket with fruits, vegetables, nuts, corn, grains, all given to us from the last two harvests. Let the produce spill out of the basket and use it as a centre piece for a meal to celebrate Mabon or place it at your altar.

☾ Hold a home-grown or local produce meal with relevant foods to give thanks to what the harvest as given us.

☾ Spells for balance, or to create calm in specific situations or in your life in general are beneficial at this time. Other relevant spells are for protection and security in the approaching winter months.

☾ Prepare for winter. Clear out your house or room and prepare your altar too. Clear out any unused items and also clear your mind, get rid of any negative situations or negative energies that you may be carrying with you. Cleanse your house at this time.

☾ Create acorn necklaces or trinkets, and bless the acorns with luck and protection for the winter months. Hang these at your altar or give them to loved ones.

☾ Take a walk into the woods; collect things for your altar and look for signs of autumn.

ALTAR IDEAS

• Light green, brown, orange and red candles. Apple, cinnamon and spiced candles are also good. The green candles represent the green earth that has passed us and the autumnal-coloured candles represent the earth and the changes all around during this season.

- Places fruits such as apples, pears, berries and autumn vegetables as offerings to your relevant deities. Collect some windfalls from the ground, and once you're finished with the offerings you can place them on a bonfire and use the ashes for future magickal workings or you can lay the fruit and seeds down in the wild for animals to eat and for seeds to grow.
- Brown, red, orange and black ribbons and cloths are great to drape and tie at your altar. Wearing these colours to honour the Sabbat is relevant too.
- Decorate your altar with acorns, pine, autumn leaves and corn.

FOOD AND DRINK

- Home-made grain breads made from rye, wheat, oats and corn
- Potatoes – mashed, roasted, etc.
- Home-grown or local vegetables, butternut squash, sweet potatoes, corn, carrots, onions and courgette
- Nuts and nut roast
- Apples, apple juice, spiced apple cake and apple cider
- Fruit turnover cake, dried fruit cakes and fruit bread
- Fresh meats or meat substitutes
- Grapes and wine
- Pomegranates

CRYSTALS

Relevant crystals to carry around with you this time of the year, to meditate with, are to use in divination and spell work, and to place at your altar are:

- Amber
- Yellow agate
- Sapphire
- Quartz
- Citrine

You can dry these herbs at your altar around this time for future use. They're amazing to use for cooking and making teas (depending on what they are and if they're edible), as well as for using for magickal workings.

- Sage
- Marigold
- Milkweed
- Rosemary
- Apple seeds and dried apple
- Camomile

INCENSE

Any autumnal/winter blends are good to use during casting circles, burning at your altar around Mabon time and for cleansing and consecrating, as well as magickal workings. Here are some specific ideas:

- Apple
- Cinnamon
- Sage
- Pine
- Fern

SAMHAIN

WHEN IS SAMHAIN?

Northern hemisphere
31 October – 1 November, traditionally celebrated from the evening of 31 October until the morning of 1 November

Southern hemisphere
31 April – 1 May

WHAT IS SAMHAIN?

The Wheel of the Year has now turned a full circle, and for Wiccans, this is their new year. This is the biggest celebration of the year for many Wiccans. Samhain is the third harvest of the year, the harvest of meat. Samhain is a celebration of those who have passed on; it's a time to honour the dead and a type of Wiccans' 'day of the dead'. It's the second spirit Sabbat of the year (the first being Beltane). It's believed that on this day the veil lifts between us and the spirit world, so there are spirits wandering the streets and it's a time to honour these spirits and celebrate the lives of our deceased loved ones. There can be no life without death; it's a part of the circle of life and the Wheel of the Year. Balance is everything, we are celebrating this, we are celebrating death itself, so it's still a joyous Sabbat, we are not sad! We are aware that life will return next spring. Darkness and winter are now taking over and shorter and darker days are here. The sun god is now making his descent into the underworld, which lifts the veil between us and the spirit world. The Triple Goddess is in her crone phase and she will now swallow the sun god and bring darkness throughout the land.

HOW TO CELEBRATE IT

Celebrations at this time of year are about appreciation, compassion, remembrance and reflection.

ACTIVITIES

☾ Divination, especially scrying, is powerful at this time of year. Because the veil is lifted, it's believed that you get a more accurate insight into the unknown and the future. You can also use scrying as a form of necromancy (connecting to the deceased); it is also at its most effective and most powerful at this time of the year. It's also actually a safer time of the year to do things like Ouija boards and seances. Because the veil is lifted and the spirit world is open to everything, not just sprits that might try to get through to you to cause harm, but also loved ones who are close at this time, so connecting with them is much easier. Show respect and don't mess around with the sprits, it will backfire.

☾ Visit a graveyard or a loved one's grave, lay flowers, pumpkins and other offerings on graves to honour the deceased. If you do this in the weeks leading up to this time, it lets your loved ones know that they are welcome to your home at Samhain.

☾ Spells to cast this time of the year are, again, the big ones. Tackle the ones that require greater power – energies that you require may be all around you, but remember to cast a circle to keep out the negative, especially at this Sabbat! Perform love spells, sex spells, protection, hope for the winter months and banishing spells for lingering negativity so that it does not enter the New Year with you.

☾ Wear black to honour the Sabbat and honour the deceased.

☾ All spirits are wandering on this day – both good and harmful. It's traditional to wear costumes to scare any negative, unwanted spirits away. Some dress as ghosts or wear white to trick spirits into thinking that they're one of them too. Some also dress as the deceased, a skeleton, ghost or ghoul to honour the dead and to put themselves in the shoes of the deceased for one evening.

☾ As it's coming to the end of the Wiccan year, renewing your altar and magickal tools at this time of the year is a good idea.

☾ Carve pumpkins and turnips. This was originally a pagan tradition; they were carved with spooky faces and left outside houses to scare away negative sprits and discourage them from entering your home.

☾ Throw a Samhain feast for your loved ones. Lay a place or two at your table and some food for those that you are remembering and place a photograph of the deceased nearby to invite them to join you on this day.

☾ To show respect to the wandering dead, you can leave offerings such as food at your door for any who might not have a place to be.

☾ This is the last opportunity to harvest your herb garden. It is bad luck to leave any crops out past this time as they are seen as offerings to the dead and it is believed this can lead to a bad harvest the next year.

ALTAR IDEAS

- Place pictures or mementos of deceased loved ones on your altar.
- To honour the dead and the Sabbat, you can also leave memorabilia in the windows of your home along with black candles to entice the sprits of loved ones into your home.
- Decorate it with skulls, or fake skulls.
- Collect animal bones or feathers to honour nature's loss and the cycle of life. After you have finished with these, remember to put them back where they came from.
- Light black, gold and orange candles. They represent the autumn and the colours of the earth at the time.
- Add autumn leaves and dead plants to your altar to honour nature's death.
- Place gourds, pumpkins and black cat figurines on and around it.
- Add crow feathers and figurines – crows symbolise death.

FOOD AND DRINK

- Meat is a huge part of Samhain as it's the time of the farm animal slaughter, but if you do not eat meat, substitutes are just as good!
- Roasted foods such as seasonal vegetables, potatoes and parsnips
- Pumpkin – pumpkin pie, seeds, breads and soup
- Corn – sweetcorn, popcorn, cornbread
- Apples – apple cake, apple pie, apple juice, apple cider
- Spiced wine, cider and mulled wine

CRYSTALS

Dark-coloured crystals are great for this time of the year. Relevant crystals to carry around with you, to meditate with, to use in divination and spell work and to place at your altar are:

- Black tourmaline
- Smokey quartz
- Obsidian
- Clear quartz
- Granite
- Amber

HERBS

You can dry these herbs at your altar around this time, for future use. They're amazing to use for cooking and making teas (depending on what they are and if they're edible), as well as using for magickal workings.

- Calendula
- Rosemary
- Apple leaf
- Bay
- Garlic

INCENSE

Good incense to use during casting circles, burning at your altar around Samhain time and for cleansing and consecrating, as well as magickal workings, are:

- Myrrh
- Nutmeg
- Mint
- Cinnamon

THE ESBATS

The Sabbats celebrate the changes of the seasons and their relationship with the sun, and Wiccans celebrate the male deity of the sun god. During the Esbats, we honour the feminine deity of the moon. The moon is seen as feminine; it corresponds with the female menstrual cycle. About every 29.5 days (roughly every four weeks) an Esbat comes around. There are usually twelve full moons in a year, occasionally thirteen: when a full moon appears twice in one month it is named a 'blue moon'. Even though the Esbats are less well-known than the Sabbats, they are just as important and are integral parts of the Wheel of the Year. The moon reaches its greatest power once a month, so that's the time of the month to do tons of different magickal workings. These full moons are the time to charge your tools and crystals and honour the goddess of the moon. At Esbat celebrations, covens often have a ritual, a feast, spell craft and socialising. We give thanks to the goddess of the moon and use the full moon to enhance our psychic powers for whatever we choose to do now.

Following is a short explanation of the Esbats:

JANUARY || THE WOLF MOON

(also known as the Old Moon, the Winter Moon or the After Yule Moon)

January's moon is an excellent time for protection, strength and planning. It is the time to look to the future. The days are still cold and dark, but they are very gradually beginning to lengthen. It can be a cold, lethargic time, when we feel out of sorts in many ways. Try to begin to think about goals that you'd like to complete for the year – write a list, keep yourself safe and try to harness positive energy. Take some time for yourself at this moon and relax, meditate somewhere warm and listen; think about what needs to be done and the changes that you would like to make for the year and ask your goddess to help you determine this. Take time to connect with yourself and your deities. Perform spells for protection, prosperity, luck and motivation. Heal yourself with crystals such as haematite. Correspondences to this moon would be plants such as marjoram, thistles and nuts; colours such as silver, black and white. Relevant trees are birch, rowan and hazel. Another correspondence would be the element of air. You can incorporate these correspondences by decorating your altar with these plants and burning hazel, rowan or birch in your cauldron to ensure motivation is high in the month to come.

FEBRUARY || THE QUICKENING MOON

(also known as the Hunger Moon, the Storm Moon or the Death Moon)

The Quickening Moon is all about new beginnings. Start to put any plans that you've made into action now. We need to clear any negative problems away and clear anything that is no longer serving you; begin to think about your happiness and whether situations, people, jobs, etc. are truly having a positive effect on your life; if not, now is time to start a plan of action to change things. Your goddess can be asked to help with anything you'd like to achieve that is relevant to this moon. Spells to cast at this time are for health, confidence, motivation, banishing negativity and also fertility, which definitely relates to this time of the year. Correspondences for this full moon are crystals such as rose quartz, jasper and amethyst and herbs such as sage and myrtle. The colours are purple, blue and silver; the element of this moon is fire.

MARCH || THE CHASTE MOON

(also known as the Seed Moon, the Crust Moon and Worm Moon)

This is the time of the year to shake off the last few months when it was difficult to find motivation and welcome the spring at full force, plant mental seeds and begin to put the plans you made over the last few moons into action. Your head may not be in the best place at this time, it can be confusing getting rid of the mental dust that has settled in your mind but, go with it, let it be and it will pass. Start to clear your spaces out and get rid of anything that no longer serves you, stop procrastinating and go for it. Also, cleanse your area from negativity using smoke; this can really help create a clear mind at this time of the year. Winter is coming to an end now. Begin to prepare yourself mentally for new exciting things to happen in your life. Spells to be cast at this time of the year are, once again, motivation spells, luck spells and power spells. Other correspondences may be crystals such as aquamarine, aqua aura quartz and bloodstone, herbs and plants such as apple blossom, wood betony and basil, and colours such as green, yellow and lavender. The relevant element to this moon is water.

APRIL || THE SEED MOON

(also known as the Pink Moon, the Wind Moon or the Egg Moon)

April often brings the rain and wind. This is the time of year to look at your career or path in life, even your path in Wicca! Look at everything and decide whether you are on the right track and if you are truly happy with where you are going. Weigh the good against the bad and decide where you see your life heading, career- and path-wise. Then take action. If you decide to change paths, it's the time to do it! April is known as the Seed Moon; so it's time to plant new seeds in any direction that you feel necessary. It's also the time of fertility, the start of conception and growth. This is one of the best times to harness the moon's energy and draw it into yourself to help with all of these changes that you may be making to improve your life and well-being. If you find all of this overwhelming and it has the opposite effect to making you feel better and more balanced, try meditating. Spells to cast around this time are for career, ambition, power, money and love, and spells for any aspect of improvement in your life that you'd like to proceed with. Correspondences for this moon are bright, motivational colours such as red, yellow and blue. Use crystals for healing and with meditation for this moon such as angelite, selenite, quartz and agate. Herbs and plants such as fennel, dill, dandelion and milkweed all relate to the element of this moon, which is air. Other correspondences are trees such as hazel and willow.

MAY || THE HARE MOON

(also known as the Planting Moon, the Flower Moon and the Milk Moon)

May's moon marks the beginning of summer for some of us, and warmer days. Growth is flourishing and it is time to get outside and feel the air, pot some plants if you haven't been feeling up to it already and carry on with all those plans you've had over the spring and winter months. This is an extremely fiery moon, where passion is flowing throughout the earth – fertility, new love and growth are all around us. This is an effective time to focus on friendships and also on relationships – if you are in one and you're happy, then celebrate the love between you both! However, it might be the time to look for a new relationship and to make changes to your love life. If this is the case and you need direction, meditation with rose quartz or the Tarot can help you find answers. Spell work around this time could focus on love, sex, friendship and fertility. Correspondences are crystals and stones such as ruby, rose quartz, amber and garnet. Herbs full of spice and fire are relevant to this Esbat, such as cinnamon, paprika and mint. Appropriate flowers are daisies and dandelions. Other correspondences are hawthorn and rowan trees. Colours like orange, red, blue and yellow are amazing too. The element of this moon is fire, as you can imagine. (Fire rituals under this moon are awesome!)

JUNE || THE LOVERS' MOON

(also known as the Dyad Moon, the Strawberry Moon and the Strong Sun Moon)

Summer is now here and the earth is green, flowers are blossoming all around! The days are getting longer and growth is everywhere! It's time to care for and enjoy your career, strive and improve where you can – work hard and you will reap the benefits! It is the same with relationships and friendships: love and nurture the people that you care about as much as you can – nurture every aspect in your life really. Ensure that you take care of your home and garden too. The goddess is mothering the fields and tending to the green earth. Maybe have your Esbat outside on this day. The Lovers' Moon is another great time to draw energy from the planet to aid you with your psychic abilities and call on your goddess to help you with spells such as self-love and confidence spells and spells to help you with anxiety and mental health. Colour correspondences of this Esbat are the colours of the sun – warm colours such as gold, yellow, orange and red. Relevant crystals are agate, yellow topaz and lapis lazuli. Herbs and plants such as parsley, mugwort and mosses are wonderful for this moon; other correspondences are trees such as oak and the element of earth.

JULY || THE MEAD MOON

(also known as the Blessing Moon, the Hay Moon and the Thunder Moon)

The sun is at its lovely peak in July and the heat is all around us, flowers are blooming and food is growing. This is an extremely joyous time and the warm weather can make us feel wonderful and positive. However, sometimes extreme heat can result in our energies being low and can make us feel a little down. It's okay at this time to be selfish in ways that benefit you, while not having a negative effect on others; it's okay to leave a relationship or friendship that isn't helping your happiness *at all*! At this time, you may feel confident enough to make some changes and take some time for yourself to rebuild your energy and discover what is making you happy and what isn't. This can be a very busy time, so it's good to take some time now to think about this and act on it now, or later. Meditate and ask your goddess for guidance. Spells for this time of the year are for a specific change that you'd like to make that is personal to you – stamina spells, beauty and career spells. Colour correspondences for this moon are silver, grey, blue, green and turquoise. Other correspondences are trees such as ash and oak and herbs and plants such as lemon balm, mugwort and camomile. Crystals for healing around this moon are opals, pearl, moonstone and malachite. The element of this Esbat is water.

AUGUST || THE WYRT MOON

(also known as the Red Moon, the Wort Moon and the Grain Moon)

August is the last push of summer before autumn rolls in, so it's a relevant time to get motivated and complete plans and strive for results. The days are beginning to get darker; it's time to thank your goddess for the success you've had over summer with spells and other magickal workings. This is the time to make good use of the remaining summer energy to get on with any new or unfinished projects. Creativity is flowing around this time so it's a good idea to channel this into something that will give you pleasure. Spells are for creativity, luck, money and protection, as the colder days beckon. Some correspondences are crystals and stones such as topaz, tiger's eye, garnet and carnelian. Colours include yellow, orange and red. Other correspondences are herbs such as rosemary, camomile, basil and catnip and trees such as hazel. The element of this Esbat is fire.

SEPTEMBER || THE HARVEST MOON

(also known as the Hunters' Moon and the Barley Moon)

September is the harvesting moon, the earth is cooling down and we are spending more time inside our homes. Our emotions can be a little all over the place, and we need to prepare ourselves and our homes for the colder months. It's also time to give thanks to the summer and the food that the harvest is providing for us. The summer might have been stressful and busy and can leave us with cluttered emotions, so use this time to clear through them, sort your life out a bit and free yourself of anything that needs to be cleared and give thanks. Cooking and kitchen magick can relax you around this time, as well as cleaning and meditation. Meditate and give thanks to the goddess for the fulfilment that the harvest is giving us. Good spells for this time of the year are for protection, luck and abundance, as well as cleansing spells. Correspondences of this Esbat are earthy tones such as brown, green, dark red and burnt orange. Crystals for healing around this time are peridot, bloodstone and chrysolite. Other correspondences are herbs and plants such as wheat, witch hazel, valerian and flax, and trees such as are birch and larch. The element of this Esbat is earth.

OCTOBER || THE FALLING LEAF MOON

(also known as the Travel Moon, the Dying Grass Moon and the Blood Moon)

October's full moon arrives before Samhain and reminds us that winter is just around the corner. The Falling Leaf Moon is the time when the hunting and slaughter seasons are near and the energy shifts critically around this time. The darker days and colder nights are here and we honour our ancestors at this time of mortality. Everything becomes crisp and bare, trees shed their leaves, animals go into hibernation and death surrounds us in many ways, but life will always return next spring! The Falling Leaf Moon is the time to honour all of our loss – of nature, animals and our ancestors. The veil is lifted between this world and the spirit world again, and this is an ideal time to connect with loved ones and ask for them to join you for this Esbat. This is the best time of the year for divination, necromancy or spending the Esbat honouring the dead. Crystal and stone correspondences are obsidian, tourmaline and onyx. Herbs and plants are apple blossom, mint and sage. Tree correspondences are apple and yew. Colours for this Esbat are black, silver, purple and blue, and the element is air.

NOVEMBER || THE SNOW MOON

(also known as the Frost Moon, the Beaver Moon and the Tree Moon)

November is here and so is the cold weather and the frost. Protection for your home and your mental state is needed. It's time to cleanse and protect our home and our emotions. We may want to protect our houses with magick and charms, or we could protect ourselves by also making sure that our career and money are looked after. It's also time to shed negativity, toxic friendships and relationships, toxic situations and have a fresh start for winter if you need it. Look for anything that may affect you during the colder months and sort it out to prevent problems. We can call upon our goddess to help protect our loved ones at this time. Draw the moon's energy down to us, meditate with it and look for changes that need to be made in order to create protection. Spells for this time of the year are protection, healing, money, luck and career. Correspondences for this Esbat are colours such as light yellow, brown, grey and dark blue. Other correspondences are crystals and stones for healing and meditation such as jade, jasper, garnet and amethyst, and herbs and plants such as fennel, cayenne pepper, betony and verbena. Branches and leaves from any type of tree can be used to place at your altar to honour the fallen of autumn. The element of this Esbat is water.

DECEMBER || THE OAK MOON

(also known as the Yule Moon, the Cold Moon and the Long Night Moon)

The December moon is the last moon of the year; it actually comes after Yule. From now on, the days will slowly begin to get longer again and the cycle will restart. New beginnings and changes will happen once again and we welcome back the sun as it gradually returns. This is the time of self-discovery and evaluation of the passing year. Look back on your year and meditate on it, call upon your goddess and ask what needs to be changed, think about mistakes that you may have made and any gains and losses you experienced, and use these reflections to improve the next year. Think about new goals that you want to aim for in the coming year. This is the time to share love and appreciate what you have. Do not dither over what you don't have but instead work for what you want. Spells to perform at this time are for peace, balance, cleansing and relationships. Correspondences for this Esbat are colours such as white, red, black and gold. Herbs and plants are mistletoe, ivy, berries, parsley, lemongrass and sage, and trees are pine, holly and fir. Crystals and stones for healing and meditation are ruby, amazonite and moonstone, and the element of this Esbat is fire, for the return of light.

15.

Altars and Magick Tools

An altar is a sacred surface, whether it be a table, shelf, small area or, for the more secretive or private Wiccans, a cupboard or chest. It is an area where we set up special tools which we use for magickal workings of all kinds. It is also a place where we come to honour our deities, the seasons, the Sabbats and Esbats, to give thanks to all of the elements and our natural world and to do things such as magickal workings and divination. Most importantly, an altar is a place to which a Wiccan can come to just be. It's a place where we can meditate and feel calm and safe. An altar is great for focusing your thoughts, especially during your practices. This is why it's important to set up your altar exactly how you like it, to make it a place that you love and like the look of and to know that you like being at your altar; this can help a lot with focusing on your practices. You don't have to spend tons of money on your altar or have *all* of the tools to begin with, nor do you have to have a beautifully decorated, aesthetically pleasing altar with lots of items on there. It can be as simple or as extravagant as you like and you can take your time building it. It doesn't make you a lesser Wiccan because you have only a few tools at your altar, because it's personal to you. You can make a lot of stuff for your altar or collect things slowly. An amazing aspect of Wicca is using the natural world to help us alongside our practices, so there is absolutely nothing wrong with handmaking objects for your altar. Also, it's important to note, anything at your altar can be remade or replaced and you can have multiples of items. There are specific times that are best to renew or remake your tools if you wish to do so, such as the Yule, Imbolc, Ostara and Samhain Sabbats, and also at the beginning or ending of the month or at a full moon. Although it is not necessary to wait for these specific times to renew tools, if you don't want to wait.

TEMPORARY OR PERMANENT ALTARS

You can set up either a temporary or permanent altar depending on how you like to work and whether it's practical. As a Wiccan, I feel it's important to have an altar because it gives me a place to be, and a place where I feel safe and where there is limitless potential. However, I am very aware that for some people, it is not possible to have a permanent altar in your home. Some may have problems keeping an altar because of the risk of it getting destroyed, others may not be able to have one because of their home life situation or you might simply not want a permanent altar and prefer to store tools and set up temporary altars when you choose to do your workings.

Some, like myself, have a permanent altar. This would typically be set up in a safe place in your home where it will not be disturbed by anyone other than you. This type of altar would normally stay put – of course, you can change it and move it around if need be, but it usually stays in one particular place for a long period of time. If you have a permanent altar, but would like to set up a temporary altar for different reasons, you can always take tools from your altar to use at your semi-permanent one, or you can keep a whole other set of tools to use, depending on your preference. As for a temporary altar, it's a lot more flexible for people who may have trouble setting up a permanent one. You can set a temporary altar up anywhere you feel is suitable to perform your magickal workings and to store your tools somewhere safe and away from them being disturbed. I like to set up temporary altars depending on the type of workings I'm doing and the location that I would like the workings to take place in.

MAGICKAL TOOLS FOR YOUR ALTAR
AND THEIR USES

WAND

Your wand is a magickal tool that you can use in your workings,
commonly made from natural, long-lasting materials such as wood,
crystal and stone. Wands are typically over 6 inches long and made
from a smoothed-down natural material, thicker at the end you hold
in your hands and tapered towards the top. There are many misconceptions about what wands actually do, *cough* Harry Potter *cough.
We do not use wands the way you have probably seen them used in
the movies. We mainly use them to channel and project energy that
comes from within us to a certain point of focus such as a specific
object or a space. As a Wiccan you can make your wand yourself, or
purchase a wand that you feel a great deal of connection to. Some
choose to have a wand made out of their birth tree or a tree they feel
a connection to, the same goes for crystal and stone wands made
from materials that you might feel an association with. If you choose
to make your own wand you can find the wood you wish to gather;
if it's not lying on the ground, be sure to ask the tree for permission
first and thank it how you please – I like to thank the tree with water or
seeds. Then you can dry the wood out, sand it down, maybe varnish
it and decorate it how you choose. You can use paints, carve or write
relevant symbols on your wand, you can add appropriate crystals to
it, feathers, string, anything imaginable that is relevant to you and
however you'd like to decorate it. Some Wiccans have many wands
they work with in their practices and some only have one, once again
it depends on the Wiccan and their personal preference.

CAULDRON

You can keep as many cauldrons around your house as you please,
as with any of these tools. I have found that it is always good to

keep one cauldron at your altar permanently because you can use them for many different workings, but I'm aware cauldrons may not always fit on your altar. A cauldron is typically an iron pot with small legs and a matching iron lid, but in reality any pot that is water-proof will do. Cauldrons are normally used for smaller workings like burning stones, oils or materials for smaller spells. For bigger workings, you may need to use an actual pot, fire pit or heated oven. (Unless you have a hench cauldron with a heated surface to place it on.) You can heat your small cauldron with a tea light candle. Like all of your magickal tools, treat your cauldron with respect and keep it clean and undamaged so that both the physical leftovers and energy from previous workings that you might create in the vessel will not affect any future workings.

BROOMSTICK OR BESOM

Unfortunately, a broomstick is not something that we ride around on, as much fun as that would be. You can keep your broomstick next to your altar or on the altar itself, depending on what size it is; it can be a full-size broom or a small hand-held one. We do *not* use our broom for cleaning our altar; this is also a common misconcep-tion. Instead, we use it to clear (*sweep*) away energy surrounding our altar that we don't want. We can do this before any magickal workings or divination. You can also use it during rituals to help clear anything that needs clearing. You can buy a broom, but it's preferable to make your own broom because manufactured brooms can include nails and glue which are believed to be bad for clearing the energy around you, as they inhibit the energy flow. So, if you do decide to buy a broom, make sure it's naturally made. You can bind your own broom using twigs that you have collected and left to dry out. Using string or rope, you must bind these twigs securely to a long, thin piece of wood, which you will also have to dry and can sand down and gloss, in a similar way to your wand. You can choose the appropriate and relevant wood for your broom in the same way that you choose the material for your wand.

ATHAME

At your altar you could typically keep two specific knives, the first being an athame. This is a type of ritual tool that you use in your magickal workings for metaphorical cutting; you don't normally use an athame for physically cutting things. You can use this knife for channelling and protecting energy, which means that an athame can also be used to cast a circle and also cutting bonds in order to be free of certain things. An athame usually has a dark handle, made out of stone, wood, crystal or metal; it is typically over 6 inches long, although some are smaller and possibly easier to work with. The athame does not have to be sharp, because it's not physically used for cutting purposes. You can make your own athame out of wood, much like you would a wand, by carving, sanding and glossing it. A lot of Wiccans like to buy their athames; you could simply purchase a knife that would be appropriate for this purpose. You can purchase your athame from online pagan shops or magickal shops, or you can look in stationery shops or second-hand shops. All you have to decide is whether it feels right for you, and if you are drawn to working with it. After you have found or made your knife you can decorate it; some like to leave the point of the dagger clear of embellishment, but once again it's up to you. If you're working with the fae, try to use your wand for the things you would typically use your athame for because the fae are repelled by knives.

BOLINE

The second knife you could keep at your altar is a boline. This is a knife you use for the physical cutting of raw materials during your magickal workings. You can use it to cut plants, herbs, flowers, offerings, etc. at your altar. It's typically made with a much lighter handle, usually cream or white. You can also (carefully) use your boline for carving your other tools. Of course, because it is used for physical cutting, the boline needs to be much sharper than your athame. Your boline can be a regular knife that you can incorporate into your workings; it then becomes a boline. Some Wiccans prefer to use crescent moon blades, small scythes or even scissors. Once again, it's best for this knife to be made from natural materials.

CHALICE

A chalice is a representation of the goddess. It is a glass, goblet, cup or even sometimes a mug made from materials such as silver, gold, metal, clay or any safe drinking material that won't leak. You can buy specific chalices from pagan shops or the chalice can be something a lot simpler, such as a stoneware cup. You can fill the chalice with water, wine or a liquid of your choice and its contents are typically used as an offering or as a symbol during rituals. Your chalice can also be used to keep an offering in on Sabbats, in order to honour your deities.

BOOK OF SHADOWS

You can store your Book of Shadows at your altar too. Some choose to keep it here just for major convenience. It can also be a good place to store it because the area of your altar usually remains untouched. (See Part 2, Book of Shadows for more information.)

DIVINATION TOOLS

You can place any of your favourite divination tools at your altar, including tarot cards, scrying tools, rune stones, tasseography teacup, pendulum, etc. This is a convenient place to keep them close to you in your most sacred space. Some Wiccans keep the tools they use most frequently there because it is believed that this keeps the tools connected to them and helps the tools get used to your patterns, which can help with divination. This can be particularly helpful with new divination tools.

OFFERINGS

You can also keep offerings for your deities at your altar. Leave herbs, relevant foods, wines and water to give thanks to your deities at the Sabbats when you call upon one to help you with a ritual, a spell or any other magickal workings. One of the most frequently asked questions about honouring your deities is what do you do with the offerings when you place them at your altar. Some believe that they should burn the offerings, leaving them at their altar for a period of time prior to this, and then using the ashes for other types of magickal workings. Others believe that you can leave your offerings at your altar for the period of time you deem appropriate and then remove them to a compost bin or bury them in the ground, which gives something back to the earth.

HERBS

Drying herbs at your altar is also a great thing to do. Why not try creating a wall hanging or some sort of shelf to hang herbs on that may need to be dried for specific workings. You can also have herbs at your altar for offerings to your deities, and each herb can be relevant to the specific deity; for example, if you're giving the offering to a god or goddess of fertility or love, you may use a herb like lavender or rose flowers.

GOD AND GODDESS CANDLES

Typically, at your altar you could have two candles — one repre- senting the goddess, female energies or perhaps the goddesses who you work with, the other the god, the male energies and any other gods in the set of deities you work with. The goddess candle usually sits to the right of your altar and is a light colour, such as gold, white or rose, and the god candle sits to the left and is a darker colour, such as red, black or blue.

STATUES

Instead of having candles, you can have statues of your main deities, especially if you have specific gods or goddesses or only choose to follow feminine or masculine ones. The statues can be made of concrete or stone and bought online or in local shops, or they could be symbols such as carved, wooden cut-outs.

PENTAGRAM

As the main symbol of Wicca, a pentagram at your altar is a good idea. The pentagram symbolises the five elements – spirit at the top, and going clockwise from there the points represent water, fire, earth and, lastly, air. These are all essential factors of the natural world; we need all of these elements of our natural earth to preserve life, which is why they are so important. Some form of pentagram at your altar can also provide protection during your practices. As Wiccans, we can use a pentagram for evoking and invoking deities. The pentagram is frequently traced or drawn out with our athame and wand. We also use a pentagram to cast circles.

The pentagram can be engraved, made out of natural materials like sticks and wood or other materials, or even bought online or from a local store. I feel like it's really important to have at least one at your altar, but you can have as many as you like – for me, the more the better!

INVERTED PENTAGRAM

In some faiths and religions the inverted pentagram is seen as evil, and unfortunately because of this our innocent pentagram that merely represents the elements of this earth can be confused with representing 'the devil'. In reality the pentagram was never a symbol of evil and before this belief came around, the inverted pentagram actually represented male energies while the upright pentagram represented female energies. Use it how you will, but in the Wicca faith it is never used to represent evil nor does it mean this to us personally.

OTHER SYMBOLS

Any symbols – engraved, made or bought – can be placed at your altar too, as long as they feel relevant to your practices or have significance to you.

BELL

This seems to be less common now but traditionally, keeping a bell at your altar was very important. A bell can be used for many things in your practices: some keep it there to use when they would like to call upon their deities. It can also be used for getting rid of any unwanted energy, as the vibrational properties of the bell clear any bad energy away. Any type of bell is good – you can buy a special bell that may have relevant symbols on it or just a regular one. Antique and vintage shops are the best for finding these at a good price. Bells made from metal are preferable.

WATER

Water is an important representation of one of the elements – that's right, you guessed it, *water*. It can also be used for spell work, casting circles and put to other uses. In a nutshell, it's a handy thing to have around you while you're working. The water can be kept in a cup or bottle, but not your chalice since you may need to use that for other things. Water collected from a clear lake, a stream or the sea can be useful because natural, unfiltered water carries helpful energy and properties.

SALT

Salt represents another element at the altar – earth. Again, this can be used for many things in your workings, including casting a circle. Many potions are made using salt as an ingredient.

SAGE

Sage is a great thing to keep at your altar – even a bunch of dried sage always comes in handy. Sage can be used to represent air, and for me, personally, it is essential for casting a circle, cleansing and many other magickal workings.

INCENSE

Incense can be used to represent air. It can be used to cleanse and consecrate tools. Also, because several scents can have relevance to specific deities, incense can be used to honour the Sabbats and deities.

CONSECRATING YOUR TOOLS

Once you purchase or make the tools you are using for magickal purposes, it's important to cleanse and consecrate them. This ensures that the tools you are using are free from any positive or negative energy that they might have picked up from wherever they have come from. The tools are then cleared and ready for use in your practices, and they get used to your patterns and your own magickal purposes. Some people choose to do this just before the first time a tool is used; others do this frequently. If the tool has been handled improperly – for example, if it has been picked up and played with by a child or has been used for negative workings – it may need to be cleansed or consecrated again. The tools at your altar can be permanently kept there, but any other tools you use are best stored in a dark or black cloth to keep out any unwanted energy or, at least, in a safe place where they will not be mishandled. They may need cleansing again before use if they have been stored for long periods of time, but it is up to you to determine whether the specific tool needs this or not.

GETTING A TOOL USED TO YOUR PATTERNS OF WORKING

Minor tools – candles, statues, water and salt – may not need this, but some Wiccans like to get major tools – wands, divination tools, brooms and chalices – used to their patterns. You could do this before you cleanse and consecrate it, or you could do it afterwards. Personally, I like to do it beforehand. This can be done by meditating with the tool or carrying it with you in a bag for between ten and thirty days, and sleeping with it near you at night. This is just the first step towards connecting with the specific tool.

CLEANSING THE TOOL

First you must cleanse the tool to rid it of any unwanted energy it may have picked up before it came into your possession; this is to ensure that anything it may have picked up will not have an effect on your workings. It's like ensuring you're starting with a clean slate.

You can cleanse your tools in many different ways. While cleansing your tool, you could say something like, 'I cleanse this tool, so it is clear and ready to assist me within my work.'

WHAT YOU WILL NEED

- Water from a natural source
- Salt or earth
- Burning sage or incense
- A lit candle

☾ Run the tools through natural water such as a stream, lake or river water. Sea water is another option, but be careful if your tool is metal or material – either dry it instantly after doing this or choose a different method for cleansing.

☾ Burn sage or incense and run the tool through the smoke it releases; do this for up to five minutes or until you can feel the energy has been cleared and it seems less cluttered. You can stop and start and hold it tightly to feel whether the energy has cleared.

☾ Leave the tool in the earth for twelve hours – some like to leave it longer depending on how old the tool is and how much energy it might have picked up.

☾ Wave it through a candle or a flame, quickly, so it doesn't become damaged. If the product is flammable you may prefer to use one of the other methods for cleansing.

CONSECRATING YOUR TOOL

1. First, start by placing the four tangible elements around you. Place the element of air to the east of you: this is sage or incense. Then place a lit candle, representing the element of fire, to the south of you. Then place water to the west of you to represent the element of water. It's better for the water to be in a chalice or cup for this ritual as it's more difficult to get out of a bottle. Last, but not least, place the salt or dirt to the north of you to represent earth.

2. To start the consecrating ritual, begin by casting a circle. I do this before I do any magickal workings if I feel the need. Since these tools are going to be a huge part of your practices, I feel that this is necessary, but if you don't, then that is completely okay. See the Spell Work chapter in Part 3 (pages 151–66) for casting circles.

3. After you have cast your circle, face east, hold the tool straight out in front of you and say, 'I choose this [name of tool] to assist me within my work.'

4. Then, close your eyes and visualise all of the unwanted energy leaving the tool – this might take a few minutes.

5. Now, turn to the south, where you will start by consecrating the tools with the elements. Start by facing the element of fire and saying, 'Element of fire, I choose this [name of tool] to assist me within my work', then bend down and pass the tool through the flame quickly, or if the tool is flammable, just wave it through the heat coming off the candle a few times. As you do this, say, 'I bless and make this [name of tool] sacred, tool of my craft, I charge this [name of tool] with the element of fire.'

6. Next, turn to face the west, going round in a clockwise direction to face the element of water. Once you face this direction, say, 'Element of water, cleanse and fill this tool I have chosen for my magick.' Then, bend down and take a few drops of water and sprinkle them over the tool that you're consecrating and say, 'I bless and make this [name of tool] sacred, tool of my craft, I charge this [name of tool] by the element of water.'

7. Then, turn to the north to the representation of earth and say, 'Element of earth, cleanse and fill this tool I choose for my magick.' Then, bend down and take a sprinkling of salt or dirt and sprinkle it over your tool, saying as you're doing this, 'I bless and make this [name of tool] sacred, tool of my craft, I charge this [name of tool] by the element of earth.'

8. Still holding the chosen tool in front of you, turn to face the east and say, 'Element of air, I cleanse and fill this [name of tool] I have chosen for my magick.' Then pass the tool through the smoke of the sage or incense and chant, 'I bless and make this [name of tool] sacred, tool of my craft, I charge this [name of tool] by the element of air'.

9. Finally, still facing east, hold the tool above your head, touch it to the floor, then hold it to your chest, stating, 'This tool is ready

to assist me within my work, being consecrated and charged, so blessed this [name of tool] be.'

10. Remember to close your circle.

After this, just work with your tool and use it as frequently as you can to see the connection between you both flowing. If you continue to work with the tool as much as you can, one day you will have bonded with it so much that you will be able to handle it a lot more loosely and even if you don't use the tool for longer periods of time, it will still be fine for use (see pages 146–7 on cleansing tools).

SETTING UP YOUR ALTAR

The way you set up your altar is completely up to the specific Wiccan. As I said previously, it needs to be set up in a way that you are completely happy with and, as your Wicca journey continues, you will discover new elements to add to your altar, changing things around and making it your own. You may even find some tools that you started with are no longer necessary and some you will come to see as being of great importance. An altar can be as simple and small as two candles, you could have an altar with only things that represent the four elements or it could be as complex and large as a table full of tools. For any of you who may be stuck when contemplating setting up your altar, below is an illustration suggesting how to kick-start the process. You will not need all of these tools to begin with.

Another suggestion, if you're completely stuck with setting up your altar, is to follow the pentagram set-up rule – that is using any item you have at your altar will have some relation to *one* or more of the elements. So, for example, your wand, because it is made of wood, can represent earth or air, so it can go to the lower left or the upper left of your altar, and so on.

16.

Spell Work

Spell work and rituals can seem complicated and mysterious to begin with, and feeling awkward is completely normal when you're starting out on the witchcraft side of your journey. As your practice continues, you will learn spells from books, online, through Wicca forums and apps. You will soon be working with your intuition, developing your own spells and rituals that work for you.

Do not be put off if a spell doesn't have the desired effects; this often needs practice and just because a spell works for one person, it does not necessarily follow that it's going to work for another. Some spells may not work at all; others may work wonderfully at the first attempt. You will soon discover a sense of doing things your own way, working with your intuition, developing your own spells and rituals that work for you.

As with many things in life, practice truly does make perfect. The accuracy and flow of your spells, potions and rituals will definitely improve with repetition and experience. However, everybody needs to start somewhere, so following are a few spells learned from close friends, in addition to some of my own personal ones to help you kick-start your spell work. There is one spell for each of the main categories: honouring spells, blessing spells, banishing or dispelling spells and gaining spells.

BEFORE YOU BEGIN

One of the most important aspects of spell work is getting in the right headspace before any spell or ritual. There are a few things that I do to achieve this and to focus my concentration before my magickal workings.

VISUALISATION

My first tip is visualisation. This helps you focus on the goal that you are planning to achieve with your spell or ritual work. Your intent needs to be heightened; you need to really want to achieve the result of the spell or ritual and you need to be sure that you have tried every other way to achieve the result before you cast the spell. With visualisation, you have to dig into the deepest recesses of your brain in order to find the subject at hand and see it in order to send the message of your intentions out into the world. This way, the universe and the earth's energies know that this is your intent. My mother is not a particularly spiritual or magickal person but sometimes, maybe once a year, when she really needed something, she would go outside and ask the universe for it, with all of her intent. And every single time she believed that, it worked. I always think of this when casting spells and doing ritual work in order to show the universe how much I need the energy for it, to show them my intention is needed. There are several ways that you can visualise. Here are some of my favourites:

VISUALISE 1 - THE BASIC METHOD

Take a walk. This is extremely good, especially when you're doing a ritual where you have to reach a destination such as a lake, field or woods, before practising your magickal workings.

I take a walk to my destination, then I lie down or sit cross-legged, I relax every part of my body completely and close my eyes. I focus on my remaining senses. I listen to every sound, to insects and animals around me, to the wind and maybe to every whisper; feel the ground below me; notice how the air smells; every little thing is heightened. Notice changes in your body, which senses react to your environment? As you relax, you can sometimes still see shapes and also make out patterns in your imagination. You can slowly begin to visualise your intent for your ritual and spell and focus. Focus until you feel you can no more – this may take three minutes or it may take thirty.

VISUALISE 2 – THE FIRE METHOD

Make your environment ready for some spell work or ritual work and sit in a place where you are comfortable. Take your cauldron or a vessel that is fireproof. Place your favourite type of wood or sage in it and then set it alight. Some people like to watch the fire; in this case ensure that you have a material that will burn continuously, or you can have a material that produces smoke if you prefer. Burn this item and focus on the fire or the smoke, keep focusing on the medium at hand; don't lose concentration. Think about how the curves of the fire or smoke create shapes, can you see your intent in the shape? Notice, how do the forms change? Keep focusing on your intent until the smoke or fire stops. Be sure to have a window open if you're doing this indoors – it can get super smoky and set off a fire alarm, in my personal experience!

VISUALISE 3 – THE BOWL METHOD

Prepare your environment so that it's ready for you to start your magickal workings and make sure that you are comfortable. Find a dark or white bowl and fill it almost full with water. Light a candle and position it so that the flames are reflected in the water, preferably to the centre of the bowl. Watch the flame in the water and, again, visualise the intent of the spell work that you are about to perform. Focus on this flame and your intent for as long as you feel necessary. This could be for a few minutes or hours; enough time for you to feel that your message to the universe has been read and understood. When you feel that the time is right, trace the shapes of a singular word that represents the intent of your spell, using your hand in the water. Touch the ground below you, then hold your hands above you and thank the universe.

VISUALISE 4 - THE MEDITATION METHOD

Meditation is another effective way to cast your intent out into the universe using visualisation. It focuses concentration and balance within your mind and body. (See Part 2, Meditation for tips.)

CREATING A SPACE

First it's important to create the best environment for casting spells, and performing rituals and even divination. Lots of changes can be made in order to help your headspace; everybody works better in their own, individual, preferred environments. Here are some tips:

☽ Adjust the heating – this depends on whether you're doing your spell or ritual work outside or inside! When you are in a meditative state or a state of heightened concentration, your body temperature can either rise or drop, so adjust the temperature beforehand to account for this.

☽ Adjust the lighting – again this depends on whether you're inside or not, but dimming your lights or using candles can sometimes help create a more effective atmosphere to work in.

☽ Make sure that you won't be disturbed. This can depend on what you're doing; sometimes you might like to involve your family and friends with spell work and make it more accessible, so this might only apply for more serious spells which require you to be on your own. In this case – be sure to ask your family, partner or anyone you live with not to disturb your concentration. Feed your animals and make sure they're comfortable elsewhere and, if you have children, ask somebody to look after them, if necessary.

☽ Put on music, a soundtrack of nature noises in the background or, my personal preference, a relaxing yoga soundtrack. Some people also like to work in complete silence; the choice is yours.

☽ Wear the correct attire. Some Wiccans have specific clothes to wear during spell and ritual work. Others just prefer to wear something that is comfortable to work and move in. For ritual work you might choose to have a cape, robe or special item of clothing saved just for these occasions or you might even choose to be skyclad (naked).

☾ Be comfortable. Wherever you are, outside or indoors, make sure you're as free and as comfortable as you can be.

CASTING A CIRCLE

Casting a circle means casting a protective space around yourself, your altar or the space that you are working in before casting a spell, or performing ritual work and divination. Casting a circle can keep out unwanted and negative energies and can strengthen and concentrate your energy too. Casting a circle can also create a safer place to be and this allows you and your energies to flow within the circle, without any outside disturbances. Some Wiccans find it necessary to cast circles for any spell, ritual or divination work, whereas some pick and choose depending on the importance of the spell that they are casting. You will soon learn what feels right for you personally. There are many ways to cast a circle and so many aspects of casting can change to suit your surroundings and personal preferences. This is my method – feel free to adapt it, as and when you wish! For example, at Mabon, I complete casting my circle by laying oats or grain around me!

CASTING MY CIRCLE

All these items will already be at my altar:

- Broom
- Incense
- Chalice
- Wand
- Athame
- Sage
- Water
- Salt

HOW TO CAST YOUR CIRCLE

1. Get rid of any unwanted air and energy in your space – take your broom, or a tool you use to replace your broom, and make a sweeping motion around the area you are working in and your altar or around the tools that you are using in whatever magick you are about to perform. There may be unwanted energies lingering in that space; just sweep them away!

2. Cleanse your circle – take your water for the element of water, salt for your earth element and sage for the elements of air and fire. In your chalice, pour a small amount of water, then add a small amount of salt, mixing the salt and water. I use my athame for this, then wipe it clean.

3. Stand facing the east, place your hand in your chalice and sprinkle the salt water around you, rotating and working in a clockwise direction. As you are moving around think about how the water is really cleansing the area, let your hands and the sprinkling of water guide you around your circle. Do this until you return to your starting point, facing east.

4. Now take your fire and air element; in this case, sage. Light the sage and assume your position facing east; once again, going around in a clockwise direction, drag the sage around your

circle, letting it flow through the air, using your hand to waft the smoke around your circle.

5. Prepare your circle – now, standing within the circle, I take the time to call upon my deities, sometimes the whole group of deities that I'm working with or a specific deity whose help I require. For example, I may call upon my deity Nuada, the Celtic god of healing, if I were casting a healing spell. To call upon my deity, I would say something like, 'Nuada, the mighty god of healing, I call upon you to watch over me while I work.'

6. Visualise – now you need to channel energy within your circle. Once again, face the east, your starting point, and begin by grounding yourself to the earth. Hold your tool (wand, athame, etc.) out in front of you with both hands and connect yourself to the earth. Close your eyes and breathe in deeply: take four seconds to breathe in and then four seconds to breathe out, slowly. Now, it's time to visualise: feel all of the energy within you rooting you to the ground below you, feel the bottom of your feet connecting to the earth below you. Visualise the energy projecting through your body, connecting the top of your head to the bottom of your feet, to the earth. Concentrate on the flow of energy that is rooting you to the earth below your feet.

7. After you have grounded yourself, now envision a light. This light is coming from under the ground below you, travelling into the bottom of your feet, up through your legs, into your chest and arms, into your hands and fingertips; you may feel a tingly sensation in your hands, then visualise this light travelling all the way through the tool that you are holding. The light might be white or gold, but everyone imagines a different colour. After you have this light radiating through you, it's time to cast your circle.

8. Cast your circle – while still facing east, still envisioning the light travelling through your tool, say the words, 'Element of air, I call upon you to watch over me while I work.'

9. Then move round to the south and visualise the white light travelling in your tool – helping you draw the circle, joining to the next element. When you are facing the south, say the words, 'Element of fire, I call upon you to watch over me while I work.'

10. Do the same and turn to face the west, still keep visualising your light and then say the words, 'Element of water, I call upon you to watch over me while I work.'

11. Then turn north and speak the words 'Element of earth, I call upon you to watch over me while I work.'

12. As you do all this, visualise the white light drawing out your protective circle.

13. Last, but not least, call upon the element of sprit. Turn to face your original starting point, hold your tool above your head, with both hands, as high as you can. Then bring your tool down, kneel and touch the ground with it and as you do, say, 'As above, so below, I call upon the element of spirit.'

Your circle is now cast and ready for your workings. After you have completed the practice that you intended to do within your circle, you have to remember to *close* it.

CLOSING YOUR CIRCLE

Kneel on the ground in the place where you finished completing your circle, where you called upon your spirit element, facing east. As you did before but, this time, in reverse, bring your tool from the bottom of your feet, stand up and bring your tool to point right above your head. Envision the beaming light from before disappearing as you reverse the circle, disappearing back deep inside of you, through your body, legs, into your feet, back into the ground and as you do this say, 'I thank the element of spirit, now I close this circle.'

Now still facing the east, hold your tool out in front of you and say, 'I thank the element of air, now I close this circle.'

Now moving *anti*clockwise around the circle, still envisioning this beaming light disappearing back inside you, turn to face the north and say the words, 'I thank the element of earth, now I close this circle.'

Then continuing in an anticlockwise direction, with the light still travelling back through your tool into your body and into the ground, face west and say the words, 'I thank the element of water, now I close this circle.'

Then, turn to face south and say the words, 'I thank the element of fire, now I close this circle.'

After that, turn back to face your starting point and thank your deities for your practice by saying something like, 'I thank Nuada for helping me within my practice.'

After finishing closing the circle, I like to just brush away the air around me again with my broomstick to get rid of any unwanted energies.

Then, you're done.

SIMPLE SPELLS TO PRACTISE

A SPELL TO HONOUR A LOVED ONE WHO HAS PASSED

Intent: To honour or to thank a deceased loved one *or* someone who left your life in some way, maybe moved away from you, for the effect that they had on your life. This will help you cope with grief and assists emotional healing.

WHAT YOU WILL NEED

- Your favourite beverage – tea, cocoa, coffee, etc.
- A picture of the passed loved one (a spare photo that you won't miss, or a copy)
- A piece of memorabilia or something that the person loved (e.g. their favourite food or drink)

- A white candle (I would recommend a thin, medium-sized candle)
- Light (matches or a lighter)
- A piece of paper, if you don't have a picture that you can write on
- A pen or marker

Method

1. Pick a day that is relevant to the person – the anniversary of their passing, a day that you frequently saw them on, or maybe an anniversary of when you met them, or maybe the next full moon.

2. Take your candle, the picture of them, the pen and the item that reminds you of them or their picture and put them somewhere you can sit comfortably.

3. Light the candle and, as it burns down, make yourself your hot beverage, then sit yourself comfortably – as you're making the drink and then sitting, think of the person you have lost and keep them in mind the whole time.

4. Sip your beverage and, as you do, write a small letter to this person, on the back of the picture or on the piece of paper. Write down things that you wished you had told them, what they meant to you, why you need to say goodbye. Sign the letter with your name and then write this underneath: 'The meaning of this spell is gone but never forgotten, or gone until we next meet.'

5. After you have done this, read your written message out loud, so if the spirit is listening it will hear it. Or, if this is for someone that hasn't passed and just isn't in your life anymore, the energy will be passed to them.

6. After doing this, continue to sip your drink until the candle burns out, then fold your picture or piece of paper as small as it will go.

7. Keep it safe and untouched then, when you can, take it to their gravestone or a place that is relevant to you both or to your memory of them. Perhaps you could also take an offering of something that they liked or a piece of memorabilia that you don't mind parting with. Bury it in the earth, lay it on the stone or near it, or place it somewhere where it won't be found.

A HOUSE-BLESSING SPELL

Intent: To bring positivity, happiness and good energy to the home. Negative energy can build through people's actions. Use this spell for a new start and to help drive away negative energies in the future.

WHAT YOU WILL NEED

- Fennel
- Basil
- Peppermint oil
- Black salt or coal and sea salt mixed together
- A fireproof dish
- A tea light candle and a lighter or match
- Sage
- A chalice
- Saltwater

Method

1. On your dish, place the tea light. Anoint the tea light with a sprig of fennel, a leaf of basil and a dash of peppermint oil and a sprinkle of the black salt.

2. Start in the entrance room of your house. Light the candle and say:

   'This house is good,
   so not its past,
   clear this room,
   let happiness last.'

Then place your candle down and clap twice in each room to clear the negative energy vibrations.

3. Do this in every room of your house. Bring the candle to each room, repeating the same words and then clapping twice.

4. Once you have finished, leave your candle at your altar to burn down – never blow it out before it's ready. While the candle is burning, stare into the flame and visualise the negativity disappearing and burning away like the flame.

5. Then, take your sage, light it, start at the entrance room and go around every room, allowing the smoke coming from the lit sage to cleanse each room. Allow the smoke to purify any negative energy that may be lingering. As you do this, in each room say the words: 'By the powers of Fire and Air, I cleanse this house!'

6. After you have done this, do the same with salt water in your chalice; start at the entrance room and sprinkle and flick salt water throughout each room. As you do this, say the words: 'By the powers of Earth and Water, I cleanse this house!'

7. After you have finished all of the rooms, say the words: 'I thank the elements for blessing this house, so mote it be.'

8. Dispose of the water in the garden or in a river.

A BANISHING AND PURIFICATION SPELL

Intent: To remove a feeling, situation or person from your life.

WHAT YOU WILL NEED

- A match
- Pink salt or sea salt
- Black ribbon
- Cumin
- A dish for burning

- A small piece of paper and a pen
- A small glass jar
- An offering or a small item that is relevant to the person/situation/feeling that you are trying to banish

Method

1. Place cumin into your jar until it's about half-full; place a spoonful of salt on top of the cumin.

2. In your dish, write on the paper the situation, name or feeling that you would like to get rid of, fold it up, place it in your dish and burn it.

3. Now, place the ashes into the top of your jar, on top of the cumin and salt.

4. Fasten the lid onto the jar as tightly as you can and then, every night before you go to bed, shake the bottle as many times as you please. As you do this, picture the situation or person moving away from you. Do this until the next full moon comes along.

5. On the day of the full moon, take the black ribbon and tie it around the top of the jar

6. Take your jar and the offering to a river, the beach or somewhere appropriate for disposing of the situation.

7. Place or throw the jar into the water and then turn your back on it. Throw your offering over your shoulder into the water too. Then walk away and don't turn back or return to the area until the next full moon arrives in the following month.

A SELF-LOVE AND RECOVERY SPELL

Intent: To gain self-worth for well-being and healing

- A small piece of rose quartz
- Salt, or pink Himalayan salt
- A rose
- A lily
- Mint
- Thyme
- 2 or 3 bay leaves
- Cinnamon
- Olive oil
- A pot to cook in
- A jug or bottle that you can seal
- Water
- A spoon

Method

1. At your stove, boil enough water to fill your bottle or jug.

2. Pick the heads from your rose and your lily and separate the petals into the simmering water.

3. Add a pinch of salt to the water, and then add the oil, the mint, the bay leaves, the thyme and the cinnamon and stir with a spoon.

4. As you are stirring the potion, say the words:

   'I forgive myself,
   and love my body.
   I accept the suffering,
   let it move forward with me.
   The light I seek has not gone yet,
   cherish who I am, and fights it's met.

I accept myself and love myself too,
let my power, continue to shine through.'

5. Repeat this three times as you are stirring.

6. Place the potion in your bottle and seal it.

7. Have either a bath or shower that evening. If you have a bath, place a small amount of this potion in the bath and hold the piece of rose quartz in your hand for the duration of time that it takes to run the bath and say the words again:

> *'I forgive myself,*
> *and love my body.*
> *I accept the suffering,*
> *let it move forward with me.*
> *The light I seek has not gone yet,*
> *cherish who I am, and fights it's met.*
> *I accept myself and love myself too,*
> *let my power, continue to shine through.'*

8. If you have a shower instead, take a small amount of the potion and rub it on your arms and hands and then hold the piece of rose quartz in your hand and say the above words, then get into the shower and wash the potion off your arms and hands.

9. You can keep this bottle of potion and use it in this way whenever you need a boost of self-love or recovery.

17.

Colours

Colours are extremely powerful; they can trigger physical reactions, affect our emotions, alter the vibrations in situations and influence the energy around us.

We are surrounded by colours from the natural world; leaves and grass can be vibrant greens, which make us feel alert and alive, and a scarlet rose will immediately draw your attention and can encourage passion and high energy.

Every colour has different associations and properties which we can use to our advantage in magickal workings. Coloured ribbons, candles and flowers can be incorporated into spells and placed on your altar, colour can also be considered in celebrations and clothing. You might also have a specific colour that you prefer to surround yourself with during spell work, or just generally in everyday life! My favourites tend to be yellow and red, because of their positive, warm, relaxed and happy vibes.

COLOURS AND THEIR CORRESPONDENCES

Red Passion, love, sex, attraction, high energy, strength, danger, war, conflict, assertiveness, power, warning

Green Abundance, growth, prosperity, luck, herbal magick, acceptance, money, healing

Yellow Warmth, energy, inspiration, happiness, success, friendship, pleasure, knowledge, growth

Blue Peace, water, protection, power, focus, luck and fortune, weight loss, harmony, spiritual release, spiritual strength, determination

Pink Romance, love, passion, care, peace, tenderness, kindness, friendship, nurturing, spiritual growth, femininity, relationships

Gold Fortune, career, health, justice, luxury, money, attraction, understanding, divination, luck, positivity, masculinity

Orange Happiness, creativity, expression, energy, fun, new start, joy, success, ambition, goals, fulfilment, overcoming

Purple Spiritual guidance, wisdom, psychic power, breaking barriers, removing evil, breaking habits, politics, luck, truth, meditation, mystery

Brown Comfort, house blessings, healing, strength, prosperity, concentration, luck, home, garden, stability, food, finance

Black Wisdom, protection, safety, banishing, reverse, scrying, defence, pride, removing curses, power, grounding, knowledge

White Purity, wholeness, peace, good, cleansing, innocence, magick involving the fragile and innocent, balance, truth, spirituality, raising vibrations, wishes, healing

Silver Psychic awareness, psychic ability, dream work, meditation, the moon, luck with risky subjects, intuition, femininity

18.

Crystals

For thousands of years, humans have been drawn to crystals, rocks and stones, believing them to have magickal properties; the ancient Egyptians used turquoise, lapis lazuli and clear quartz for healing and protection. Wiccans use these amazing and beautiful products of our natural world to help with endless aspects of their magickal workings, healing, meditation, spell work and even for divination. Each crystal has its own individual energies and vibrational properties. In a sense, they work the same way that plants do; having plants around your house can affect your mood, your mind and your body, according to the type of plant and its properties. Having crystals throughout your home and carrying crystals around with you can affect your moods in different ways and can also help with spiritual, mental and, in some cases, physical healing.

USING CRYSTALS IN WICCA

Meditating while holding specific types of crystals cannot only help focus your thoughts, but also if you have something particular that you'd like to meditate on, you can use a stone that has properties that relate to the issue. This will help to give clarity to your thoughts and to guide you.

You can use crystals within spell work too, and within rituals; you can use them to create or change something or even infuse potions with them.

Crystals can also be used for healing and protection. Some people choose to carry specific crystals around with them or wear them as jewellery – pendants and talismans, for mental protection or even manifesting energy towards you. For example, wearing rose quartz may gradually bring feelings of love towards you, while sunstone is perfect for summer and bringing warmth, happiness and positivity.

You can also leave crystals around your home for protection. Some people even use crystals for psychic healing, and use the properties within crystals to heal their bodies or minds, calming anxiety and helping balance their emotions. This can have extremely effective results; for example, to soothe a sore throat, holding fluorite against it can calm the pain, and amethysts are good for combatting sleeplessness. (**Note:** Even though crystals help with many ailments, do not rely on crystals as a cure; they are a tool to help but always consult a doctor if you have concerns about your physical or mental well-being.)

Also, crystals can be used within divination, to concentrate energies and to make divination tools such as rune stones, pendulums and scrying mirrors and crystal balls.

HOW TO CLEANSE YOUR CRYSTALS

Crystals hold energy; they collect the earth's energy (which is what makes them so magickal), but they also collect energy from people. This can be a very positive aspect when it comes to using crystals for divination, as it can make them so amazingly bonded to a specific person. However, if crystals are new to you or if they have picked up other energies, it's probably best to cleanse them before you incorporate them into your magickal workings. You can cleanse them as frequently as you feel is necessary. Here are a few ways to cleanse your crystals.

☾ Burn sage and allow the smoke to cleanse the crystal – hold the crystal and wave it around in the smoke of the sage. (You can also do the same with incense.)

☾ Hold it through running water – natural water sources are most effective; waterfalls, lakes, streams, the sea and rivers. Some crystals are *not* suitable for water so do your research before proceeding.

☾ Bury it in earth for twelve hours.

☾ Use a bell – chime the bell near the crystal a few times and knock the vibrational energy out of it.

☾ Quickly pass the crystal through the flame of a candle, again be careful with this method. It's extremely effective, but not all crystals like it!

☾ Leave the power of the moon to cleanse your crystal – lay it outside for the night in a safe place and allow the moon's natural energies to charge it.

☾ Some people use their breath to cleanse their crystals by gently blowing on them.

☾ You can meditate with the crystal and use your intuition to clear it!

CHOOSING CRYSTALS

I know when I need a new crystal as I tend to sense it. I then go and have a good look around the shops near me that sell crystals. I might see one that I have looked at before which hadn't previously interested me, but now feel drawn to it. Likewise, I might look at a crystal that has the appropriate properties relating to something that I specifically need help with. I always handle the crystal and see if it feels right. Sometimes, I am attracted to a crystal although it doesn't seem to relate to anything that I am thinking about at that time, but it often turns out to answer a future need that I was not aware of when I bought it. You can also get the same sense of being drawn to a crystal by looking at them online, so don't worry if there are no crystal shops near where you live. I have bought some of my absolute favourite crystals from online shops. See Resources, pages 226, for some of my favourites.

CRYSTALS AND THEIR PROPERTIES

There are tons of different crystals, stones and rocks that you can use for your magickal workings – so many that this entire book could be filled with just this one subject. Over time, you will discover more and more about which crystals assist you best for which purpose. To begin with, we will start with the common crystals used for spell work, meditation and divination. Here are a few guidelines about stones and their relevant uses:

A – F

Abalone shell – calming and stress-reducing
Agate – healing, soothing and concentration
Amazonite – truth and harmony
Amber – protection, healing and soothing
Amethyst – calming, aids sleep and physical and emotional healing
Angel aura quartz – harmony, peace and spirituality
Apatite – success and clarity
Apophyllite – instinct and intuition
Aquamarine –reflection, meditation and wisdom
Azurite – intuition, clarity, relaxation
Black tourmaline – balance and positivity
Bloodstone – energy and well-being
Blue agate – healing, calming and communication
Blue quartz – calming and organisation
Carnelian – creativity and confidence
Celestite – reduces stress
Chrysoprase – happiness and mental well-being
Citrine – concentration, positivity and success

Clear quartz – health, healing and clarity
Diamond – creativity, energising, self-confidence and
commitment
Dumortierite – physical healing, cerebral power, spirituality
and positivity
Emerald – healing, love, faithfulness and friendship
Fluorite – concentration, balance and cleansing
Fuchsite – communication, strength and recovery

G – K

Garnet – energising, protection and courage
Goldstone – detoxification, intuition and inner strength
Haematite – positivity, balance, concentration and
stress-reducing
Jade – protection, positivity, good fortune and independence
Jasper – strength, healing and sexual energy

L – P

Labradorite – determination and intuition
Lapis lazuli – learning, strength and prosperity
Malachite – peace, empathy and energy
Mookaite – nurturing, peace and confidence
Moonstone – stability, calm, insight and creativity
Obsidian – protection, truth and forward-thinking
Onyx – constancy, balance and resilience
Opal – creativity, positivity and soothing
Pearl – calming, stability and purity
Peridot – optimism and attracting love
Pyrite – protection, health and well-being

Q – U

Rhodochrosite – positivity, calming and encourages love
Rhyolite – healing and moving forwards
Rose quartz – love and forgiveness
Ruby – protection, courage and happiness
Sapphire – wisdom and mental well-being
Selenite – healing, protection and luck
Serpentine – soothing, confidence and cleansing
Smokey quartz – protection and converts negative energy
Sodalite – communication, calming and self-esteem
Spirit quartz – detoxification, spiritual growth and
    connecting to others
Sunstone – cleansing, healing and creativity
Tiger's eye – decisiveness, luck and mental well-being
Topaz – healing, happiness, truth and joy
Tourmaline – balance and healing
Turquoise – healing, protection and good luck

V – Z

Zircon – healing, wisdom, protection and spirituality

19.

Herbs and Plants

For thousands of years, herbs have been used for their medicinal, symbolic, culinary, cosmetic and aromatic properties. Because herbs have been relatively easily available, they have been the basis of many home-made treatments such as mint tea for an upset stomach and lavender as an antiseptic and to help induce sleep. Used in the correct way in magickal workings, herbs can have very powerful effects.

Herbs are commonly used to create potions, to consecrate items, to bathe in, for burning and for physical and mental healing. You can also make teas and drinkable herbal remedies, use them in tasseography, a form of divination, and you can cook with them. Cooking involves adding relevant herbs for the reason that you've chosen to do the spell. Some people even carry herbs around with them in a bag to bring different elements to specific situations.

Similarly, hanging different herbs in your home can attract elements into your space, as well as being specific to your preferred deities. Others may be used to calm and relax your home.

You can buy herbs from local shops. It's best to buy them with roots, in pots, so you can use them freshly picked and dry them for a later date if needs be. (Some can only easily be found in dried form, however.) It is really fun to grow herbs in your very own magickal herb garden, which can be as small as a few pots on your kitchen window sill or an aesthetically pleasing herb wheel in the garden.

It's really important to consider the natural world when using, eating or picking anything from it. This is something that you will come across frequently throughout Wicca. The best plan is that whenever you take something, give back by watering the area, planting new seeds in or around the same place or, if this is not possible, plant some seeds somewhere appropriate. Also, please be aware that some plants are protected and should not be taken from the wild under any circumstances.

Never be greedy – only use what is necessary – keep balance in mind and always leave some for the earth. Herbs are incredibly important and powerful and can be used within magick with amazing results. Obviously, there are thousands of different herbs growing around the planet, so listing them all would be impossible and there are always new ones to discover and use in different ways, which is both exciting and overwhelming.

Plants have numerous correspondences and uses in magickal workings – I have listed a few, but there are so many so please do some research and try things out to see which ones work for you.*

A - F

Basil – love, good fortune and joy, helps nausea, anxiety and headaches

Bay – promotes extrasensory power and expels negative energy

Burdock – protection, healing, detoxifying, helps skin problems

Caraway – loyalty, memory, general health, antibacterial and helps digestive problems

Catnip – love, good fortune, helps constipation, anxiety and sleeplessness

Cayenne – protection, digestion, antibacterial, helps painful joints

*Caution: Some plants may be poisonous or harmful if eaten. Please research the herb thoroughly – some are only useful as incense, essential oils or for use in magickal workings. Please also be aware that even if something is safe to eat in small amounts, too much of it might prove toxic.

Cinnamon – strength, spirituality, good fortune, passion, antioxidant and antibacterial

Clove – friendship, new love, keeps secrets, energy-boosting, antiseptic, anaesthetising

Cocoa beans – intuition, creativity, antioxidant, healing, mood-boosting

Cumin – protection, loyalty, helps digestion

Dandelion – purification, positivity, antioxidant, antibacterial

Devil's shoestring – protection and good fortune

Dill – protection, good fortune, helps digestion, menstrual problems

Dragon's blood – protection, wound repair

Elder – calming, prosperity, liberation, berries for immunity, flowers for sinuses

Eucalyptus – protection, cleansing, decongestant, antiseptic, antibacterial

Fennel – sexuality, strength, anti-ageing, menstrual problems, lowers cholesterol

Flax – prosperity, healing, psychic abilities, antioxidant, anti-inflammatory, helps menopausal symptoms

G – K

Galangal root – money, digestion, rheumatism

Garlic – protection, purification, circulation, immune system, detoxification, antioxidant

Ginger – self-assurance, sensuality, helps nausea, anti-inflammatory and antioxidant

Ginseng – good fortune, desire, attractiveness, anti-inflammatory, stress-reducing, helps sexual dysfunction

Hawthorn – fertility, purification, heart stimulant soothes throats

Hazel – antioxidant, healing, protection and knowledge

Hibiscus – passion, liberation, peacefulness, speeds
    metabolism, lowers blood pressure and cholesterol
Honeysuckle – passion, good fortune
Hyssop – expectorant, purification, protection and positivity
Jasmine – desirability, good fortune, skincare, antidepressant
Juniper – protection, antibacterial, antiviral

L – P

Lavender – cleansing, healing, joy, romance and helps sleep
Lemon balm – passion, achievement, calming, antioxidant
Lilac – love, exorcism, creativity
Marigold – respect, soothes skin, helps menstrual pain
Meadowsweet – luck, happiness, calming, helps indigestion,
    headaches and colds
Mint – energy, helps nausea and digestive system, soothes
    throats
Mugwort – sedative, purification, stimulates psychic ability
Myrtle – cleansing, antiseptic
Parsley – passion, divination, fertility, anti-inflammatory
Patchouli – soothes bites and stings, calming, aphrodisiac
Pepper – banishing, bravery, antibacterial, antioxidant
Peppermint – divination, sleep, purification, helps nausea,
    settles stomachs, helps colds
Pine – fertility, good fortune, stamina, pick-me-up,
    expectorant

Q – U

Raspberry Leaf – protection, love, regulates hormones, induces labour, clears skin

Rose Petal – beauty, romance, weddings, protection, decongestant, aphrodisiac

Rosehips – good fortune, peace, love, laxative, immunity, renews skin

Rosemary – clarity, cleansing, breaking spells, healing, respiratory, improves memory

Rowan – clarity, divination, digestion, immune system

Sage – strength, wisdom, cleansing, helps indigestion, soothes throats, anti-inflammatory

St John's Wort – protection, healing

Salt – cleansing, purification, healing, attracts energy

Sandalwood – healing, protection, positivity, calming

Seaweed – good fortune, detoxification

Skullcap – clarity, exorcism, restorative

Thyme – purification, calming, helps aches and pains

Turmeric – passion, fertility, digestion

V – Z

Valerian – calming, aphrodisiac

Vanilla – happiness, energy, love

Vervain – protection, balance, love, cleansing

Violet – luck, love, calming

Walnut – divination, understanding, concentration, creativity

Willow – inspiration, identity

Witch hazel – optimism, courage, psychic powers

Wormwood – banishing, protection

Yarrow – healing, love, divination

20.

The Witches' Alphabet

The Witches' alphabet is a secret alphabet that witches, Wiccans and pagans can use to write spells, codes, important notes and messages they may want to keep secret and not reveal to anybody who does not have knowledge of the Witches' alphabet. This alphabet is commonly used in a Wiccan's Book of Shadows and in Grimoires. The symbols used are believed to possess immense power and to have magickal properties and, for several centuries, witches have used this alphabet as their own. The actual origin of this alphabet is uncertain but there is evidence that it was used in the sixteenth century in *Three Books of the Occult Philosophy*. This alphabet can be very helpful, especially to those who do not want to reveal their practices to anyone else, particularly if you are practising Wicca or witchcraft secretly. The alphabet is sometimes referred to as 'the Honorian alphabet'. You can write it in the same way as you would write regular letters, positioning them side by side, or you can write them descending down the page, which makes a sigil. There are tons of different alphabets and symbols that people like to use to keep their workings hidden, so you can choose whichever ones most appeal to you or none at all, if you do not wish to.

The Witches' Alphabet

A B C D
E F G H
I J K L
M N O P
Q R S T
U V W X
Y Z

Another commonly seen alphabet is the runic Elder Futhark alphabet. This is seen on the rune stones used in divination. These symbols are also believed to have extremely powerful properties when using them to write, for spell work and messages.

The Elder Futhark

21.

Astrology

Astrology can be an important factor in Wiccans' lives. It is becoming increasingly popular in the modern world, although it has been around for centuries. As we have discussed, Wiccans live by the natural world, which includes the sun, the moon and the stars.

The position of the stars and planets in relation to the sun can have an effect on us in many ways; it can determine our temperament and our mood and can be used to tell the future. There are twelve sun signs, or zodiac signs, and yours will depend on the position of the sun at the time of your birth.

People who are born in the same period of time as someone else can have similar personality traits and yet two people with different astrological signs can clash or can work together incredibly well. We can exhibit other qualities from other signs, especially if our birthday is close to the end of our sign's cycle. Each sign also relates to one of the elements – earth, air, fire and water – and these, again, can affect your personality and your relationships with other people.

There are lots of correspondences relating to your astrological sign that you may be able to use to your advantage in Wicca. For example, earth signs might find strength from growing and using herbs and plants and might find meditating beneath trees particularly beneficial or easy. You could also work with your relevant element in rituals, for example fire signs might make particular use of relevant candles. You can also work with your personality traits, for instance, Geminis might be happier in a coven than being solitary Wiccans.

SUN ASTROLOGY SIGNS AND THEIR CORRESPONDENCES

ARIES

Date for sign: 21 March – 19 April
The Ram
Planet: Mars
Crystal or stone: Diamond
Colour: Red
Herb or plant: Paprika
Element: Fire

Aries are strong, competitive, driven and have great ambition. They can also be extremely short-fused and independent. They work best alone or in complete charge of aspects of their life and don't have a good temper for those who don't want to work as hard as they do. But their energy is pure. They are generous and bright, like the element they relate to. It's always good to have a friend that's an Aries as they are always there for you, loyal and respectful, but they will be upfront and honest with you too. If you give them the friendship they deserve and treat them with respect, they will return it.

TAURUS

Date for sign: 20 April – 20 May
The Bull
Planet: Venus
Crystal or stone: Emerald
Colour: Blue
Herb or plant: Rosemary
Element: Earth

Taureans are overly stubborn, which can be a blessing and a curse. They have strong desires, and once they have their mind set on something, they are willing to do whatever it takes to achieve their goal, which makes them good workers too. They can fall hard in love or not care at all. They hate dishonesty and will do anything to avoid people that are not honest with them. They have an incredible bond with nature and prefer to spend their days alone or with one or two close friends. They love indulging themselves in food and luxuries, sometimes a little too much, and can sometimes be lazy if they let themselves slip into bad habits. They do not like people who are overly negative and will steer clear of them like the plague.

GEMINI

Date for sign: 21 May – 20 June
The Twins
Planet: Mercury
Crystal or stone: Pearl
Colour: Yellow
Herb or plant: Lavender
Element: Air

Geminis have an extreme passion for keeping busy and like to stay focused and involved in every task they have to hand. They are incredible at visualising and are very good at planning and keeping things organised. They are extremely clever and enjoy education in some form. They are also fun people who love to make others laugh and enjoy being surrounded by lots of people at once. They have a wide circle of friends and never like to be alone, especially when it comes to being in a relationship or partnership. Sometimes Geminis cannot be trusted with secrets and gossip, but they always have others' best intentions at heart.

CANCER

Date for sign: 21 June – 22 July
The Crab
Planet: The moon
Crystal or stone: Ruby
Colour: Violet
Herb or plant: Balm
Element: Water

Cancerians are extremely sensitive and emotional, they tend to take everything to heart and always put others before themselves. This can sometimes make them vulnerable, so many like to build an imaginary wall to protect themselves from getting hurt. Cancerians are extremely sentimental people who like to keep old close friends near them and they like to know that their possessions are kept safe. They love caring for others and love children and nurturing animals too. Cancerians are natural healers, who have a special connection to the goddess.

LEO

Date for sign: 23 July – 22 August
The Lion
Planet: The sun
Crystal or stone: Peridot
Colour: Orange
Herb or plant: Heliotrope
Element:: Fire

Leos are fiery people who like to be in charge; they love being in control and like to have things their way. They have a short temper and trust themselves and their instincts in everything they do. They work hard and excel in their careers. Leos are naturally smart and love to soak up knowledge in their studies and their hobbies. They are also extremely picky about their friends, but make them easily, are dedicated and stick with friends for life. They have a high energy rate and love to bounce around and explore, but they also love relaxing and being lazy sometimes too.

VIRGO

Date of sign: 23 August – 22 September
The Virgin
Planet: Mercury
Crystal or stone: Sapphire
Colour: Grey
Herb or plant: Fennel
Element: Earth

Virgos are extremely practical, clean people who can't stand mess, untidiness, anything unsanitary; they can be very uptight about this. They can sometimes be very critical of others who don't share the same opinions. Otherwise, they are very down to earth and are also very sensitive to situations. Virgos are wonderful at organising and will always be the friend to arrange trips and meetings with their companions. They love the countryside and greenery and love to spend time in the garden in the summer.

LIBRA

Date of sign: 23 September – 22 October
The Scales
Planet: Venus
Crystal or stone: Opal
Colour: Purple
Herb or plant: Sage
Element: Air

Librans are creative, passionate and have a spark of excellence. They love to love and to receive love. If Librans don't have love returned to them they can be extremely sad; it takes a lot longer for Librans to get over relationships than any other sign. They have huge ambitions for the more creative careers and love to entertain and spark people's interest. Librans are always there to help anyone who needs it and are very loyal at keeping promises and secrets. They love living the fast life and spending money on irrelevant things, but this brings them joy and they manage it the best they can.

SCORPIO

Date of sign: 23 October – 21 November
The Scorpion
Planet: Pluto
Crystal or stone: Topaz
Colour: Indigo
Herb or plant: Heather
Element: Water

Scorpios are irresistible. They love sex and passion, and always have a fantastic sense of style. They are admired by many people and have lots of people lusting in their direction, but they are extremely loving to partners and others that require attention in their life. Getting on the wrong side of a Scorpio can be a huge mistake; they hold grudges and remember everything, which can be a disadvantage to people who have let them down in some way. They are very charismatic and love to be at the top of their game. They can be jealous, competitive and dominating but, to the right person, loving and protective.

SAGITTARIUS

Date of sign: 22 November – 21 December
The Archer
Planet: Jupiter
Crystal or stone: Turquoise
Colour: White
Herb or plant: Elder
Element: Fire

Sagittarians are extremely cultured, knowledgeable and well-travelled. They love to explore, go on holidays and experience the world. They enjoy learning new things and leading busy and successful lives and they get bored very easily. They hate liars and must discover the truth in everything. Sagittarians have expensive tastes, but believe in working hard to obtain the things that they want. They can sometimes be selfish and not think about others before they think about themselves, but always keep their loved ones in their heart. They can be very strong, but once you upset them, they can take your comments to heart.

CAPRICORN

Date of sign: 22 December – 19 January
The Goat
Planet: Saturn
Crystal or stone: Garnet
Colour: Black
Herb or plant: Comfrey
Element: Earth

Capricorns are always full of life; they radiate positivity and beauty, and often look younger than they actually are. They love to challenge themselves within their passions, which can make them competitive. They love having a safe and secure environment at all times and can sometimes put their guard up to people before they get to know them. They love to have fun and be silly and make jokes and are often known as 'the funny one', while still being organised and good at getting things done. Everybody loves Capricorns; they are very easy to fall for and people often want to be around them all of the time.

AQUARIUS

Date of sign: 20 January – 18 February
The Water Carrier
Planet: Uranus
Crystal or stone: Amethyst
Colour: Pale blue or aqua
Herb or plant: Thyme
Element: Air

Aquarians are lone wolves. They are very independent and love to work alone and be alone very frequently; they don't deal well with a lot of people, but still like to have many friends to see individually. They can sometimes be controlling and love taking the reins on things. They can be very jealous and sometimes just need someone to be around to make them relax. They drive themselves to greatness and don't need others to motivate them. They hate it when unfair situations hit them and believe everybody should be truthful and fair.

PISCES

Date of sign: 19 February – 20 March
The Fish
Planet: Neptune
Crystal or stone: Aquamarine
Colour: Green
Herb or plant: Parsley
Element: Water

Pisces are prone to psychic abilities. They are good at adapting to people and are good with social media. They also love to get away from the crazy world and take a break every so often to retreat. They are not always the best at dealing with situations and can become unnecessarily angry and upset. They are also creative and like to heal and care for the ones they love. Pisces are wonderful at forgiveness, but can hold grudges against people who have done them injustices. They are always looking for something new and do not settle for anything less than perfection within their relationships, careers and hobbies.

22.

Small Changes

Jumping into Wicca can seem to be extremely complicated and overwhelming to begin with. Where do I start? Which tools do I need first? What do I learn about first? Which path should I follow? For me, the key to starting off your Wicca journey simply and effectively (I wish I had done it this way!) is to take gradual steps, to dip your toe into it rather than trying to jump in with both feet! Make small changes in order to learn about your faith gradually, enjoy it, savour the wonderful aspects of Wicca, all of the time remembering that as it slowly becomes part of your everyday life it is the most positive, interesting, natural, genuine path that can help your well-being too.

Following are some small changes to adapt your life to Wicca at the beginning of your journey.

CELEBRATE THE SABBATS AND ESBATS

One of the first and most effective changes to make to your life is to begin celebrating the eight Sabbats and twelve main Esbats. This can be very easy for a number of reasons. First, many of the holidays that you may already celebrate, such as Christmas, Easter, Halloween, etc., are actually adapted from the pagan holidays, Yule, Ostara and Samhain, which are the ones that Wiccans celebrate. They are on (or around) the same date and are celebrated in some of the same ways.

So, instead of being celebrated because of Christian beliefs, we call them by their original names and celebrate them in the traditional way by honouring the seasonal changes.

If you have family and friends who are not Wiccans, then the Sabbats can tie into their celebrations too; you won't feel isolated from their holidays and rejoicing, even though you are celebrating for different reasons. Focusing on the celebrations is also an extremely fun way to learn about the Sabbats (and Wicca!). It is also relevant to spell work and the understanding of what Wicca is all about. Learning about the cycle of the Wheel of the Year and the Wiccan calendar is also a good starting point in understanding the faith.

CREATE A BASIC ALTAR

Another good way to start your Wicca journey is to create a basic altar (see pages 136–50). This gives you a place you can come to if you're feeling lost; somewhere to just be and feel grounded. Start by collecting or making the basics: a pentagram, maybe two candles to represent the god and the goddess, and also four things to signify the elements, such as, salt, water, sage or incense, and a candle. Create a small area on a desk or a shelf to begin to incorporate Wicca into your life visually. You could also add your first form of divination to your altar. I would recommend starting with tarot cards; even though I'm aware that every Wiccan has their own preferred methods of divination, the cards can be easy to start with because they are easy to understand and most have a booklet with meanings and explanations included.

READ

The most important thing that I advise new Wiccans to do is *to read, read, read* and *research*. It's important to learn about the history of Wicca and to be sure that you feel this is appropriate for you, before you go any further. It's always important to read up on any subject within Wicca before you put it into practice. Wicca is, of course, about discovery, and we shouldn't be scared of anything within it, but that doesn't mean we should just skip the reasoning behind what we are learning. Prior research can help with the accuracy of your workings, improve your judgement and minimise time wasted. I would recommend, to brush up on the basics, taking about half an hour every day, or a few hours at the weekend, to read around a new subject. Frequent, short bursts of research are easier to find time for and to get your head around. There are so many subjects to learn, so pick one aspect of Wicca that appeals to you, explore it and practise it, and it will soon start to fall into place. You will also learn about which parts of the faith are the most important and relevant to you, and those are the aspects that you will want to invest most of your time into. Even now, I put aside time nearly every day to learn something new in Wicca. There's so much to learn, you'll never stop!

PRACTISE SPELL WORK

Starting the witchcraft side of your journey can seem scary and extremely intense. Don't panic! I would always recommend starting off with small spells (see pages 160–6) to dip your toes into witch-craft. Divination is always good to practise to begin with, but basic, easy, non-intense spells are amazing too. A good example is learning how to cast a circle (see Part 3, Spell Work) and maybe just practise achieving the flow of casting your circle, opening and closing it. Then it won't feel as though there is way too much to think about when you do decide to do your first official spell or ritual.

An old friend once taught me how to do spells during cooking and baking, which ended up being the best way to kick-start my spell work because it was incorporating witchcraft into some-thing that was a normal aspect of my everyday life. So, it could be something as simple as maybe cooking for a friend who is having troubles with their career and adding some ingredients that have relevance to luck and power and motivation. You could say some-thing along the lines of, 'I cast only hope and luck, bless these ingredients to help be unstuck, forward now this spell will take me, for once is done I will be where I'm meant to be.'

Other spells that you could incorporate into aspects of your day-to-day life that won't feel too strange could be creating potions for your baths or maybe lotions to apply to your skin. An example of this could be if you need to increase romantic aspects of your love life, you could create a lotion or bath potion with herbs relevant to romance, such as rose, camomile and lavender, etc.

FIND YOUR PATH

One of the greatest things about Wicca is that everyone practises the faith differently. There are so many different beliefs and practice methods that it gives people the opportunity to do things their own way within the faith. A small change to make at the start of your journey is to begin to look into paths you feel you may be interested in. There are so many to explore and discover. A good start would be to look at different 'types' of Wiccans and the teachings they follow and think about which deities you feel connected to. This can help give you a direction to explore an identity within Wicca. This will help your confidence and motivation. If you don't know what 'type' of Wiccan you are and can't decide, that's totally fine too! Some Wiccans prefer to be without a 'type', some discover at a later date and some may follow one Wicca path and a particular set of teachings for a year and then change. As a Wiccan, you are free.

KEEP A JOURNAL

Documenting your progress as a Wiccan can be very important; it's a good way to keep track of what you have achieved and to look back on for future reference. You might not want to start your Book of Shadows or Grimoire when you're first starting out, you might want to wait until you have got into the swing of things. Keeping a casual journal allows you to record experiments, experiences, thoughts, changes you have made and ideas for further research and future practice without the pressure of the significance of recording in your Book of Shadows. It keeps the process more loose and casual as many Wiccans, myself included, are very precious about their Book of Shadows.

JOIN THE WICCA COMMUNITY

This is totally optional and, once again, can seem slightly scary if you're jumping into this and, of course, it's totally okay if you'd prefer to keep your Wicca journey to yourself. You can immerse yourself in the Wicca community in a number of ways: you could join pagan, Wiccan and witch apps, Facebook forums, Instagram pages or just speak to people you know who may be in any way 'spiritual'. They may know more about paganism or Wicca than you think and they may have other friends and connections to people who can help you. If you live near any crystal or pagan shops, the people who run and work in them are usually interested in the things that they sell and are also in a good position to meet Wiccans. Never feel pressured to speak to anyone about your faith, if you don't feel comfortable doing so; it took me years to speak out. It can be helpful to talk to others who may have been practising the faith longer than you and also to other newbies for tips and to share experiences. I learned a lot of what I know about Wicca from a kind woman who I once spoke to in (of all places) a pub!

A FEW WORDS OF CAUTION

Wicca is an amazing faith and there is so much to be excited to experience within your journey. As I mentioned before, the learning never stops and you have a new, positive focus for many parts of your life. It's wonderful and empowering and it can open your eyes to a new world; there is nothing to fear about Wicca or the witchcraft that comes with the faith. However, saying that, there are a few things that new Wiccans need to bear in mind; it is easy to get caught up in the wonderfulness of Wicca and forget its true meaning.

IT'S A FAITH, NOT AN AESTHETIC

If you are getting into Wicca because it is trendy, a fashion state-ment or perhaps you are hoping to gain from it in an unhealthy way, Stop Now! Wicca is very powerful and the power that comes with it can have a greater effect than you think. If you are casting spells for the wrong reasons, joining Wicca with less than good inten-tions and taking the faith too lightly, it will backfire. It's totally okay to enjoy the witchy, Wiccan aesthetic without actually practising Wicca if that's the aspect of it that appeals to you. However, the foundation of being a good Wiccan has nothing to do with having to dress, look and decorate yourself and your surroundings in a certain way. It's about using what you've got, being who you are and about your intent. If your intentions are not reflecting the right causes, that energy will come back to you.

DON'T LET THE POWER GET TO YOUR HEAD

As I said before, Wicca is incredible and can make you feel very powerful. When you are casting spells, with a bit of experience and success, it can be extremely liberating. Sometimes, that power can easily cross a line and be abused. Balance is key: magick is a gift from the earth, the lord and the lady, it does not make you *any* better than anyone else nor does it give you the authority to make decisions that you are not meant to make. You are not a god and you have these gifts because the earth has given you magick. Remember the law and its teachings – we are all equal, Wiccan or not.

DON'T BITE OFF MORE THAN YOU CAN CHEW

Wicca is a very exciting faith; sometimes it makes you feel like you want to know everything and do everything *right now*. This mentality can lead to biting off more than you can chew, casting spells you may not be ready for, draining your energy, making mistakes and rushing through important elements of your journey that would benefit from a slower approach. Remember, if you're serious about the faith and you know that you're 'meant' to be a Wiccan, you can spend the rest of your lifetime enjoying this journey. I honestly believe that you can never ever know *everything* about Wicca; even some of the most powerful and experienced Wiccans that I have met tell me that they still haven't made a dent in all that they could know about Wicca. It's like thinking that you could know everything about the entire universe! It doesn't make you any less of a Wiccan if someone knows a spell that you don't or knows how to palm-read and you don't. It's a gradual process and you will get there in your own time. Patience and practice are key.

BEWARE NEGATIVE ENERGIES AND SHADOWS

Wicca is nothing to be scared of – we can conquer pretty much anything with our intent, the natural world and our five senses. There can sometimes be 'disturbances' to your practices; negative energies and spirits can occasionally interfere. These could be sprits and energies known to this world or they could be a 'friend' radiating negativity, which disturbs the outcome of a ritual or spell. They can latch onto that energy that you are emitting from your aura. Some intrusive energies can even push past your circles and some come if you conjure them, letting them in. Summon them – why would you? So, be careful while casting spells while you are feeling low or negative or angry, these energies and sprits can feed off you. Sometimes they can come if you've had a day when you're feeling sad and maybe don't even realise you're too low to cast a spell and you can feel them attacking your circle. If this does happen, be sure to banish them or if you have nothing else at hand, at least cleanse the area before closing your circle or continuing what you're doing. This is why it's important to be in a neutral state or in a good mood while doing magick. You are more powerful than these energies and shadows; they can be scary but they are still nothing to fear and should not stop you from practising magick.

23.

When Others Don't Accept Your Faith

When you embark on your Wicca journey, even in this day and age, it is inevitable that you are going to be misunderstood by some people. Wiccans and witches all over the world have to deal with misconceptions and hostility because of a long history of an extremely warped portrayal of witches.

Over the years, I have had countless experiences of comments, both in person and online, from people who are confused and uneducated about Wicca.

Television shows, films and books about fictional witches, as enjoyable and harmless as they are, are often mistakenly taken to be a true picture of the Wicca path. I've often met people who expect me to use my wand in the same way as Harry Potter, swishing it in mid-air to make a chair levitate. Other misconceptions can be more harmful, such as the idea that we all sacrifice animals, worship Satan, want to cause harm to everything and everyone, hate all Christians and are damned, evil people. In reality, Wicca teaches the complete opposite of this fiction. The faith creates an understanding of the universe that helps you to love and respect and have compassion for everything and everyone.

Another major misconception is around the use of the pentagram, which is, of course, the main symbol of our faith. To Wiccans, the pentagram simply represents the elements, but it has been misrepresented in the media and many people think that it is a symbol for worshiping Satan or all evil.

I am also often told that our Wicca faith somehow goes against other people's belief in their 'god'. Wiccans are in no way hostile to other people's religious beliefs. We accept that everyone has the right to their own ideas and philosophies and that diversity makes for an interesting and healthy society.

WHAT TO DO IF PEOPLE DON'T ACCEPT IT

It's important not to become angry or annoyed; the general lack of understanding is just part of life and you will become used to it. However, there are a few things that you could try:

☾ First, educate. If you just come out and say, 'I'm a Wiccan and I practise witchcraft', it can sometimes be a shock to people close to you. Maybe explain the basics of what being a Wiccan means and especially what the witchcraft side of Wicca entails. Find a good article or website to show them that demystifies the misconceptions about Wicca. Often, people are more tolerant and less prejudiced once they have the facts – and realise that you're not trying to be Harry Potter!

☾ If you feel comfortable enough, maybe show them what you actually do, possibly something as straightforward as a cooking spell or some divination, which tons of people who don't declare themselves as witches would also do. This can help show how harmless and positive your practices are.

☾ Show them what other witches and Wiccans are actually like. People often have a preconceived mental image of what witches and Wiccans look like and how they (don't) fit into society and daily life! Sharing YouTube videos, pictures from Instagram and blogs by your favourite witches and Wiccans who are successful, positive and compassionate will show that your aspirations in Wicca are not dangerous.

☾ And lastly, *the most important one*: normalise it. Yes – Wicca is exciting, powerful and, in many ways, far from normal, but it's sometimes best to treat it like it's not really a big deal. This can then calm someone close to you who may feel confused or overwhelmed about the idea that you are practising witchcraft. Maybe you could show them some of the elements of what you do in witchcraft that are very similar to things that they might do on a day-to-day basis. For example, so many people enjoy growing their own herbs and plants and they might regularly make home remedies from these, such as mixing lemon, ginger and honey together to soothe a sore throat. Many non-Wiccans also wear precious stones as pendants and rings because they have special sentiments, memories or meanings attached to particular types of gemstones; which is a similar concept to the way that Wiccans might wear an amethyst on a pendant or keep one in their pocket for protection. These examples are obviously different to creating a spell or potion with intent, but the actual foundation of what many people do as superstitions, for fun and to relate to elements of the natural world is not really *that* far from mixing a potion and casting a spell.

☾ Another example of normalising your practice would be explaining how and why you have an altar. When people enjoy a hobby, such as playing an instrument or painting, they collect materials and tools connected to and for use in their interest and often get satisfaction from displaying symbolic, useful, sentimental or treasured items. Again, the comparison has flaws, but it can help others to see that your actions are not so unusual.

Unfortunately, however you try to explain your faith, some people will never accept it. For whatever reason, you might find that your choices affect others enough for them to even ask you to stop practising Wicca or they may not want to be in your life any more. Some may not even be willing to listen to your reasoning. All you can do is explain why it's important to you and the positive effects that it has on your life. If neither of you are willing to compromise, you will both have difficult decisions to make. Sometimes you just have to accept that people will never understand it, don't argue; just move on. At the end of the day, as a Wiccan, you are the living proof of what Wicca is all about – show the world how a really awesome, fair, kind Wiccan looks and acts. After all, you don't need everyone's acceptance in order to do what makes you happy.

COMING OUT OF THE BROOM CLOSET

Coming out of the broom closet is a term that means coming out as a witch or a Wiccan. At some point, you may decide that you want to be open about your spiritual path, as many people enjoy sharing major parts of their lives with close friends and loved ones. You may feel that your secretive practice is like a weight on your shoulders that you could do without. This can be a major decision for some Wiccans who are uncertain what sort of reaction they will face.

I'm very fortunate in that my family are very open and accepting to whatever I do to improve my well-being and even though they don't always understand parts of my practices, they trust me and respect my decisions. You will invariably get mixed reactions when you do actually come out of the broom closet. People close to you might be interested in finding out more, or they may be indifferent and really not bothered, worried about you (probably because of misconceptions), cross that you have been hiding this from them or they may be extremely emotional, upset or even angry.

It's completely your decision whether it's possible, at this moment in time, to come out to your family and friends; you may not even see it as a big deal and just treat it as a normal, everyday conversation.

If you're worried about this, I would recommend maybe explaining it as a nature-based religion – because it is! Make sure to try to be as respectful as you can, particularly if you are discussing it with anyone who has extreme religious beliefs or deep-rooted principles against witchcraft. It's sometimes difficult to swallow your pride and not shout and scream at the top of your lungs when people refuse to accept your beliefs, but sometimes – and you might be pleasantly surprised – it all works out for the best and allows you to continue your path within Wicca in a more open way. It's important to remember that some people will have never heard of Wicca; respect this and explain it in the best way that you can!

24.

Wicca on the Sly

Unfortunately, not everyone is able to be open about their Wicca journeys. As with other faiths, you might find that Wicca is misunderstood or unaccepted by either your family, friends, your community or maybe by people who follow other religions. Even though you may be certain that Wicca is the correct path for you, you might find yourself having to keep your practices private, either temporarily or permanently. This can be extremely challenging. If you have experience of this and can share your stories with other Wiccans who might be going through similar prejudices, be sure to speak to them and be there for them as much as you can. Having someone to talk to can help in so many ways if you feel isolated and misunderstood. You might just want to keep your faith quiet because you feel that it is nobody else's business – and, of course, this is totally fine too!

WHY ARE YOU KEEPING QUIET?

It is a good idea to think about *why* you are keeping your Wicca practices quiet. Is it completely necessary? Consider whether you are keeping your faith quiet for *you* or for someone else.

Having to keep this quiet from your parents is one of the most difficult challenges. This is made even harder if you live with them. They might follow a different religion, they might not agree with witchcraft or you could even be afraid of them teasing you or not taking you seriously. If you feel comfortable enough, it may be worth having a conversation with them about Wicca, discussing what it's all about and why it makes sense to you and explaining how it brings you positivity and happiness. If you are certain that they won't accept it or think that they may not be open-minded enough for a discussion, then you might have to accept that it will be necessary to keep your Wicca journey quiet.

If you are keeping this quiet from a partner, again, ask yourself why you are doing this. Is it completely necessary or are you just assuming that you already know their reaction to your choices? Really consider why you feel this way and whether it makes logical sense. If at all possible, take a deep breath and talk it through with them. Your partner should be supportive, understanding and listen to what you have to say about subjects that are important to you. If Wicca benefits you, then it also really benefits your partner. If you are in an unhealthy relationship situation, please think about getting professional help, or at least talking to someone that you can trust, especially if it is jeopardising your well-being.

If you are keeping this quiet from friends, again it's important to consider why. Maybe you just feel that they wouldn't understand or they would judge you. It's important to note your friends should be supportive, especially if they care for your happiness and health.

WAYS TO PRACTISE WICCA ON THE SLY

So, for some reason, you have to hide your Wicca journey in your home? Here are some ways to get around hiding your practices or making your practices more subtle.

HIDING YOUR ALTAR

First, hiding your altar doesn't have to be as difficult as you think; there are lots of different ways that you can still carry on with your Wicca practices without having an altar on show.

Having a temporary altar is probably the best option; setting it up when and where you need to. You can have your tools maybe hidden in a portable bag that you can lock, such as a rucksack with a padlock, handbag or a small case. The downside is that you may have to have fewer tools and, obviously, you might have to actually take them everywhere with you. You could also have a set of altar tools that you keep at someone else's house, if you know someone that you can trust with this. Another way of hiding your altar tools is in plain sight. I know that sounds weird, but why not? It can be the easiest solution. Many people have candles, incense holders and herbs in their house, right? You could also have some of the more unusual tools around in plain sight as ornaments, just maybe make sure that they don't have symbols on them.

MAGICK ON THE SLY

Magick can be a little trickier, just because it requires attention, care and time.

I would recommend performing it in public places, parks, fields, woods and maybe even friends' homes, if they don't mind. These all work wonderfully and I would recommend doing magick outside as much as possible. Obviously, this can be more difficult when the weather is cold, especially in the UK where it's cold for *at least* half of the year. You can also practise your magick when you're home alone or in any space in your house where you can be private and not disturbed for a period of time.

HIDE YOUR BOOK OF SHADOWS

Hiding your Book of Shadows or Grimoire can also be quite easy. Simply acquire a diary that appeals to you and use that instead, ensuring that you place a lock on it. If you feel the need to protect the contents of your Book of Shadows, you can write in symbols or use a secret alphabet (see pages 180–2).

DON'T WAVE IT IN OTHER PEOPLE'S FACES

Even though not being able to express your faith freely can be very frustrating, sometimes practising it in subtle ways, in a less confrontational, more respectful way will help to keep the peace in your household. As much as you might want to walk around with *'I'm a witch, get over it'* on your T-shirt and make your house into a Wiccan's dream lair, with pentagrams and herbs galore, a little compromise can go a long way.

Remember, this may just be a temporary situation. If there is something that actively becomes a problem and really bothers you, it's in your power to make a change; it's not your fault that people refuse to accept your choices. No matter what the reason for keeping your faith quiet, consideration, discussion, patience and time usually sort most problems!

25.

City Wiccans

I grew up in the countryside in a beautiful house, surrounded by herbs, flowers, trees and home-grown fruit and vegetables. We lived on the edge of a small, rural town, so I've been lucky enough to have practically everything that I need for my Wicca journey on my doorstep. However, last December I moved to the city, not really realising what I would be sacrificing by leaving the country-side. Yes – the city is great, there's always something interesting to do, a fantastic variety of places to eat and pubs around every corner. But, being a Wiccan in the city gives you a lot of new challenges and I have definitely discovered that the countryside is where my heart is. Saying that, in the modern world, so many Wiccans live in cities and it's most certainly very possible to make this work, even if we don't have everything readily available on our doorstep.

SITUATIONS THAT MAY AFFECT YOU AS A WICCAN

☾ Not having a garden, or an outside or green space of any sort nearby, can make it more difficult to collect the materials that you might need for your magick.

☾ Polluted air in the city can affect your health and the growth of your plants. This problem can also affect your ability to see the moon and the stars; which makes it harder to draw energy from the moon.

☾ It can be more difficult to find the privacy that you may need for witchcraft and other magickal workings.

☾ Living and working in a city and being constantly surrounded by activity, noise, concrete and a higher-density population can build anxiety and drain your energy.

☾ There are so many exciting and interesting diversions in a city – a full-on lifestyle can sometimes leave you with little time, energy or motivation for witchcraft.

☾ Living in accommodation with rules that don't allow candles, animals or hanging items on walls can limit your magickal practices.

TIPS FOR CITY WICCANS

NOT HAVING A GARDEN OR LIMITED SPACE FOR GROWING

☾ If you have a small garden, you can definitely work with it to create everything that you need. A courtyard garden, finished with gravel, could be turned into a tranquil space with statues of your favourite deities and maybe a water fountain for a calming energy. You could also decorate your space with protective amulets. Or you could easily fill it with pots, crates and other creative containers and make a mini herb garden. You could include smaller pots of some of your favourite flowers, fruit and vegetables to use in your practices. It may also be worth placing netting on top of the plants in order to protect them from neighbourhood cats. If you are worried about toxic fumes affecting your edible plants, you may want to grow them inside on window sills.

☾ If you do have a garden, plant flowers that encourage bees, butterflies and other insects. A bird table providing food and water will encourage birds too. A small pile of dead wood in a shady corner or a home-made bug house will encourage mini-beasts. Making your garden wildlife-friendly can really make you feel in balance with the natural world – even in the middle of a city.

ℂ If you have room for an inside garden, there are still lots of ways you can work around growing your own produce. You can keep potted plants all around your home, as long as you take good care of them and research into the correct conditions to help them thrive, such as which temperatures they need, whether they require direct sunlight and how much water they need to keep them strong and healthy. Good, low-maintenance plants are cacti and succulents such as aloe vera and herbs such as basil and parsley. Some of them can be used within spell work but just having plants around you can improve your mood and make you feel that the natural world is closer to you. Herbs kept by your windows are relatively easy to take care of, although most herbs last longer if grown outside in the warmer weather. Bay, sage, mint, dill, oregano, rosemary, tarragon and chives are just a few of the herbs that can be eaten and used in magickal workings. Again, look into any specific requirements that help these plants to thrive, but most herbs are not too fussy and you should easily and relatively cheaply have a display that smells amazing and is also really useful. You can attempt to grow so many different plants in your house, but sometimes it's not that simple, or possible to cultivate the exact materials that you need for your magick.

ℂ If you are unable to grow your own, you may have to source your herbs and other plants from elsewhere. One amazing answer (time and funds allowing!) is to look into renting or sharing an allotment. They are often controlled by your local council or a charitable organisation. For a relatively small amount of money, you lease a section of land to grow almost any produce and flowers that you choose. You have to be fairly hands-on and look after your plot and be respectful of the other growers and their gardens, but if you gain satisfaction from growing things on a bigger scale, this is a fantastic way to grow produce to eat and to use for your magickal workings. You will, however, often find that there is a waiting list for city allotments.

☾ A good thing about living in the city is that there are plenty of markets and shops *everywhere*. Lots of places sell a fascinating variety of fresh herbs that you can purchase as and when you need them for magick. You could buy a bunch and if you have lots left over, dry them for later use. You can just hang these around your house. Pre-dried herbs and pre-packaged fresh herbs are also absolutely fine too. Yes, using your own plant can increase accuracy, and your own personal energy through the ingredients and tools, but your intent is always the most important factor in your magickal workings.

NOT HAVING A PLACE FOR OUTSIDE MAGICK

☾ If you have a small garden, it can be difficult to do spell work here, especially if it's communal or not very private. You can still use your garden for magickal workings, just maybe on a smaller scale. Focus on what will be possible for your garden; maybe you could bring a couple of tools outside to set up a temporary altar and do smaller spell work. Maybe there are parts of your garden that are more secluded and you could perform your magick there.

☾ If you don't have a garden, you can still do outside magick; it may just take a little more effort and organisation. First, there are always parks and areas of greenery in every city. Doing small-scale spell work in these places is possible. Pack up what you need in a compact wooden box or matchboxes and find a quiet place to settle down and concentrate. If you have a balcony, this can be a huge benefit; outside spell work will be just as effective and you can work with the moon. If you're really struggling and, like me, you feel that you need privacy to be able to get the best out of your rituals and spell work, particularly for bigger spells that require lots of space or a connection with the moon, it might be worth travelling for these. There are often little-used and hidden places, even in cities; ask around and do some research. Towns and cities often have woods and fields, lakes and quiet areas on their outskirts, maybe just a bus- or train-ride away. It may take a bit of searching but you might just find the perfect place to do all of your outside magick. Please also remember to ask permission – never trespass. Similarly, always make sure that someone knows where you are going – do not put yourself in danger by going out into remote areas alone.

☾ Some people may not want to work outside and prefer to work in the comfort of their own home and that's okay too! Everybody's magick is different; we all work in different ways and some of us simply prefer inside magick and have found that's how we work best! Many Wiccans may not require the elements of what the outside gives us.

MAKING TIME FOR YOUR FAITH

If you go to university, study or have a full-time job that requires travel or takes up a lot of your time, it can sometimes be difficult to prioritise your Wicca journey. But this does not mean it is impossible. If you are just starting out in Wicca, try to schedule time into every day; even if it's just half an hour to write in your Book of Shadows or to practise reading your tarots or research a new subject. There's no need to rush, you will be working on this for the rest of your life and you will have more time for it as you continue on your journey. There's no need to pressure yourself; it's not a chore and should be fun!

If you have been doing Wicca for a while and suddenly have a change in location – maybe you have begun university, moved home or started a new job – do the same: schedule a time for your practices or even use it to wind down in the evenings before you sleep. This can be a super effective way to enjoy Wicca and make the learning element less chore-like – just chill and look forward to it in the evenings. Remember that sometimes you may be so busy that you barely have time to sleep, let alone practise Wicca, so don't punish yourself. Remember that you live and breathe your beliefs, if you miss a full moon or forget a ritual that you had planned, don't worry about it, it will come round again soon!

If you have a job that takes up a lot of your time, you can take magick with you, whether it be a book to read in your lunchtime, a form of divination you can do on the train, crystals to use for meditation or even a semi-permanent altar, as small as a match box with a few herbs, a candle and a few other mini items! Lunchtimes are always great for spell work. Find a quiet spot where you can concentrate; this may take some getting used to but it will become more natural the more that you practise.

If you share a house with friends or flatmates who take up a lot of your time and personal space, it may be awkward explaining that you need quiet time to concentrate on something that they may not understand. You could lie and say that you need privacy for a phone call or to practise meditation but it's often better to be honest with people and explain what you are actually doing. That way they won't think that you just don't want them around. Again, it's easier said than done, but if you treat your faith as a completely normal thing to you and don't make a big deal out of it, it's usually received in the same way.

RESTRICTIONS BY TENANCY OR HOUSEHOLD RULES

If your tenancy agreement doesn't allow lit candles, this can be incredibly difficult as many spells require them. Even casting circles or divination can sometimes benefit from the use of candles. You need to remember that Wicca and magick are all about working with what you've got. It's about using what is at hand and about your intent, not about items that you have purchased. For example, if you feel that you need items to represent fire, incense can often be substituted, as can herbs that you can burn and some crystals. If you are not allowed to burn anything indoors, you can always just use visualisation and concentration: all you really need for a spell is yourself!

Also, living in the city, it is unlikely that you will be allowed to or have space to have bonfires for celebrations. A wood burner or a fireplace that you are permitted to use is a good substitute. These can both be used in spells that incorporate burning and for festivities on the Sabbats.

BENEFITS OF BEING A CITY WICCAN

Even though it can be amazing to practise Wicca in the country-side, there are still some benefits to being a Wiccan in the city.

☽ One of the positive things about living in the city is shops! Chances are you are in a great place for crystal, herbology and pagan shops and can benefit from the expertise and enthusiasm of the shop owners. You will almost certainly also have easy access to markets and shops selling the extras that you may need, such as candles, symbolic ornaments and also fabulous specialist and second-hand bookshops. There are tons of individual shops you can enjoy discovering and exploring to help you with elements of your journey, and you shouldn't have to go far to find them.

☽ There is no need to feel isolated – cities are also good places to meet other Wiccans. Living in the middle of nowhere can be amazing for peace and quiet, but if you are just starting out in Wicca or want some company from other likeminded people, busy cities are the best places to find this. Larger towns and cities often have an eclectic population with a diverse range of faiths, cultures and viewpoints. I found Wiccan friends by getting to know the people who work in a local pagan shop; they also told me about pagan festivals and gatherings in the area. Another good idea is to join Wiccan forums; they are an easy way to connect with local people with similar interests and beliefs.

☾ There are more events in larger towns and cities that may involve pagans, Wiccans and witchcraft, such as Pagan Pride and spiritual festivals which are fantastic places to meet people and to buy items for use in your magickal workings. These events might also provide opportunities to learn more about your path.

☾ Sometimes particular areas of cities have a creative buzz and an intense and positive energy which can help your creativity and motivation. This can help your magickal practices and also sometimes lift your general mood!

☾ You are less likely to need a car, with more readily available public transport and paths everywhere. This is not only good for the natural environment, but also can help you connect with your surroundings. Cities are also good places to get some exercise and feel in tune with your body. There are loads of opportunities for walking and for finding a relaxing and strengthening yoga or pilates class. These activities are good for your mental health, your body and your spiritual connection. You also might be inspired to go out and find things that you usually wouldn't look for and interact with new elements and with different people that are outside of your comfort zone.

☾ Many cities have fabulous botanical gardens that promote conservation and encourage education on many interesting and unusual plants. Visit your local one when it is not too busy and enjoy the surroundings. Many also sell rare plants.

☾ No matter where you are, magick is all around you and within you. Don't let the tall concrete buildings make you feel less magickal, look for the greenery, the life and the positive energies; they might be a little harder to find, but they are always there.

26.

Small Spaces

Thinking about the space that you might have is relevant to a practising Wiccan, for instance when it comes to casting circles, performing rituals and a place for your altar, etc. In reality, we all have different-sized homes, rooms, outdoor spaces and many limitations in the areas in which we can work effectively. Spaces to live and practise in can be temporary or more permanent and some lifestyles necessitate constant travel. Also, Wiccans can start their journey at any age, with some maybe sharing a room with a sibling or possibly away from home for chunks of time at university or living with housemates without much privacy. Some Wiccans could have children and have the risk of their tools being damaged or constantly moved. Any of these limitations could feel like they affect your practices, but they don't have to. Wicca is about working with what you've got, not about how big your house or garden is, your age, background or your income; if you have the right intent, a tiny room is enough. Here are some ideas for working with the space that you have.

☾ First, have a good clear-out of any clutter, even smaller rooms feel more spacious and calm after you have got rid of any items that have no significance to your current life, or that you no longer have a use for.

☾ Downsizing your tools is perfectly acceptable – having fewer candles, maybe just two to represent the god and the goddess, a pentagram and four other items to represent the elements can be enough. You don't need an expansive array of tools for an effective altar. Try placing your altar in a drawer, on a small wooden shelf or box; this takes up less room and gives you privacy too. You also don't need to store large amounts of herbs and other ingredients for spells. You can purchase small amounts when and where you need them. Any leftover ingredients can be stored in used, cleaned medicine bottles, sealed cups or containers that can be kept out of sight. Also, it's always worth looking into spells that don't require herbs. There are so many different raw materials and tools that you can use for magick, not all of it is greenery or from the natural world. Look for spells that maybe require smaller objects or tiny amounts of herbs; it may take you in a different direction and give you the experience of other kinds of magick.

☾ If you share a room with someone, a drawer or box that can be put away under the bed, for your belongings, altar and other personal items, is a good start. Setting up a temporary, portable altar could be the most convenient way to go. Locks may also be necessary for journals, books and boxes, as privacy will probably be important to you and some people naturally may let curiosity get the better of them. As for your actual space for casting spells, you don't need a huge area, just somewhere that's big enough to sit comfortably. You can sit and cast your circle with the elements close to you and simply draw the circle out at arm's length. Also, it's not always necessary to physically mark your circle out – you can simply cast your circle in your mind. As for the best times for your workings, either wait for a time when the other person you share a room with is not around or is in a different room for a long period, which might create more space and enable you to concentrate! There might be a different room in your house that is available for you to use; you can keep a sacred space in a room other than your own room. If you have no other option – for instance, if you are in shared accommodation at university and privacy and space are limited – you can always go outside to practise in parks and public spaces (see above). Natural surroundings can have an incredibly positive affect on your spells and rituals.

☾ It is also worth talking to siblings or housemates that you share a room with. If you explain and show them what you are doing and they see first-hand the positive benefits of your practices, they might be more tolerant and less likely to interfere or disturb you and your tools.

☾ Being a practising Wiccan with children and pets can be tricky because obviously many parents do not like to restrict their children from exploring, even around objects that may be precious to them. In this case, a temporary altar in a portable container or wrapped in a cloth could be preferable. It can be removed to a high or secure place when not in use. Oils and incense also can be toxic to pets and children, so always ensure that they are burned in a room where you can open a window after use to let the smoke blow away and keep them in a locked or high cupboard otherwise. Potentially dangerous items such as your athame, boline, food offerings and candles for burning at your altar must always be used with care and safely store afterwards.

As with everything, be respectful, kind and show understanding to those around you and usually all that will be reciprocated.

27.

Finding a Coven

A coven is a unified group of witches, Wiccans or pagans which teaches and follows a specific path. The teachings are often passed down through generations. This knowledge includes whichever traditions are relevant to that coven. They often also come together for rituals, spell work and to celebrate the Sabbats and Esbats. Covens may focus on the teachings of traditional British Wicca and other established paths, but in the modern world there are many different types of covens, following a range of paths, such as Faery Wicca, Green Wicca and even Draconic Wicca! Most members usually practise and learn by themselves as well, but this would usually be along similar lines to the teachings that their chosen coven supports.

In a few covens, all the members live together, but this is much more rare in the modern world of Wicca. You usually have to be invited to join covens and they're not always easy to find unless you know someone who is already a member. Typically, you would be invited to join a coven, accepted and then initiated. After that, there may be strict rules that you will be expected to follow. There may also be one shared Book of Shadows, or Grimoire, for all. Covens sometimes operate with a High Priest and Priestess who lead, and a system of levels of initiation – you probably need to be comfortable being part of a fairly strict hierarchical system if you join this type of group. There are also many covens now that are willing to allow people to join if they have the desire to learn their teachings. They may still have High Priests and Priestesses that look after the entire coven and you may still meet up for celebrations, etc. There are also covens that function partly or entirely online, such is the modern world!

IS A COVEN RIGHT FOR YOU?

Some people begin Wicca really wanting to join a coven; this may be the right path for you because you like to work and learn within a group and it can benefit your practice when you are surrounded by people with experience and knowledge. As most covens have been practising for several generations, the teachings can be incredibly insightful. Many covens are extremely welcoming, inclusive and encouraging. You also can build a close bond with your coven members and enjoy the sense of community within the group, and you can also build amazing friendships with like-minded people.

Some Wiccans also believe that performing rituals alongside other people can help you attain a greater connection with the divine. There are covens for pretty much any path that you may be interested in but it's not always easy to be initiated, and every coven has different requirements for initiation.

Of course, you don't have to be in a coven; it's completely your choice and it doesn't make you a better or a lesser Wiccan. I have met tons of Wiccans who have been solitary their whole lives and who are incredibly powerful and insightful. I've also met Wiccans from covens that are just as intuitive and happy in their choices.

There is also something called a 'circle' – which is like a coven, but is a group of Wiccans that join together occasionally to perform ritual and spell work, celebrate the Sabbats together and share their teachings too. That's more of a casual arrangement.

Unfortunately, there are covens that believe their way is the only correct way, but that's not true. Saying that defeats the point of what Wicca is all about: Wicca has no right way of doing things. I have also occasionally heard of egotistical and petty clashes within covens – and if you come across this, try to steer clear of such behaviour, if you can.

If you are able to find a coven that suits your beliefs and in which you feel comfortable and empowered and you agree with their rules and ethics, then it may certainly be the right path for you. Even though I love being a solitary Wiccan, if I found a coven that felt just right for me, I would definitely take up the opportunity to join.

WAYS TO FIND A COVEN

Finding a coven is probably not as hard as you think. It may just be a case of getting to know other Wiccans who practise in this way. Don't be shocked if they don't tell you any details about their practices, because some covens are sworn to secrecy. You might be able to find people who used to be involved in a coven or perhaps you can research via online groups, forums and apps. If you make yourself known in these communities and prove yourself to be an active, committed Wiccan, they may even seek you out! You can always try befriending the Wiccans you know in your area who may have hinted that they are in a coven and find out more about their group in order to see if it suits your beliefs. You can also go to festivals, such as Pagan Pride and spiritual festivals, where there are opportunities to speak directly to members of covens and discover more about them.

ONLINE COVENS

You can find online covens through Wiccan groups, Facebook forums and even apps. There are lots of websites that give you contact numbers, emails and details for covens which you might be interested in joining. Pagan councils can also help you search. If a particular coven does not accept you, do not be discouraged or disappointed; this does not mean that your practices are deficient in any way. You may just not be quite right for their particular group in some aspects of your practice or you may need to complete their requirements before joining, which may just take a little more work!

Last Few Words

Over the last few years my journey into Wicca has been life-changing. It has definitely helped me develop and grow as a person, helped me to enjoy life more and I truly believe that I wouldn't have been able to face some of the challenges that life has thrown at me without it. I've learned a greater level of respect for the earth and for the others sharing it with me. I've also found that my gradual developments in practising witchcraft – and incorporating this into how I live – have brought a whole other level of power to my existence.

Some of the most incredible people I have met over the last few years have been Wiccans and pagans, who have helped me learn and challenge myself within my journey and given me the strength to grow and learn from others, both within the faith and outside, who might not be as kind or understanding. The actual practice of Wicca has been going on quietly for centuries, flourishing and becoming more widely known since about the 1950s; now, it continually evolves to fit into the twenty-first-century world. We have as a community overcome barriers of how Wiccans, witches and pagans are seen, and have flourished and used our faiths and practices to make our lives the way we want them to be. As Wicca is taken into the modern world, our growth will continue and our practices will evolve. However, the foundation of Wicca will always be as pure and as gentle as it was at its beginnings. Even in this modern world, our beliefs will always be to follow the sun, worship the moon, talk to the trees, listen to the plants, swim in the water, light the fires and breathe in the air, for as long as our earth is still spinning.

Blessed be all the Wiccans, witches, pagans and others x

Resources

BOOKS

Wicca by Scott Cunningham
Living Wicca by Scott Cunningham
Earth Power by Scott Cunningham
The Modern Guide to Witchcraft by Skye Alexander

ONLINE

www.thehoodwitch.com – this is a fantastic blog full of posts on everything from fashion to music, and the Sabbats to Tarot.

www.wicca-spirituality.com – another wonderful resource for articles on all things relating to Wicca.

www.wiccadaily.com – an online channel for all your Wiccan news, articles, photos, rituals and spell guides.

www.witchfest.net – the largest organiser of witchcraft festivals in the world, this is a great resource for finding a Wicca-based event near you.

YOUTUBERS

Anaïs Alexandre
BehatiLife
Eadig
Laura Daligan
The White Witch Parlour

INSTAGRAMMERS

@behatilife
@downtostars
@thehoodwitch
@wiccamovement
@witchradio
#wiccapath

SHOPS

Every Witch Way
www.everywitchway.co.uk

The Goddess & The Green Man
www.goddessandgreenman.co.uk
17 High Street, Glastonbury, Somerset BA6 9DP

The Hoodwitch
www.thehoodwitch.com

Innanas Festival
www.facebook.com/inannamagicNORWICH
2 St Andrew's Hill, Norwich NR2 1AD

KrystalRealm
www.etsy.com/shop/KrystalRealm

Wicca Daily
www.wiccadaily.com

EVENTS

The Norwich Mind Body Spirit Festival – this is a great way to meet other Wiccans and like-minded people. There are plenty of exhibitors all of whom are there to help you with finding spiritual enlightenment. The festival takes place every June in Norwich.

Pagan Pride UK – celebrating and raising awareness of modern Paganism, this non-profit organisation organises an amazing annual festival in central Nottingham on the first Sunday of August.

The Stonehenge Solstice Festival – a music festival like no other! Specially located in the Salisbury Plain, this is the perfect event making friends and enjoying its uniquely relaxing and magical atmosphere. It takes place annually, during the Summer Solstice.

About the Author

Harmony Nice is a twenty-something YouTuber and Instagram star helping to bring a greater interest and understanding of Wicca to a modern, diverse audience. She became interested in Witchcraft and Wicca at the age of fourteen after discovering that her great-grandmother, Hilda, was a witch. Three years later she started her Youtube channel to communicate with other practitioners, educate newcomers and generate discussion. She appeared on the BBC documentary 'Britain's Young Witches' in 2017.